History of Spain

A Captivating Guide to Spanish History, Starting from Roman Hispania through the Visigoths, the Spanish Empire, the Bourbons, and the War of Spanish Independence to the Present

Free Bonus from Captivating History
(Available for a Limited time)

Hi History Lovers!

Now you have a chance to join our exclusive history list so you can get your first history ebook for free as well as discounts and a potential to get more history books for free! Simply visit the link below to join.

Captivatinghistory.com/ebook

Also, make sure to follow us on Facebook, Twitter and Youtube by searching for Captivating History.

Contents

Introduction

Throughout the centuries, Spain has been subject to the lordship of other countries. It was occupied by the ancient Greeks and Romans, the Visigoths, the French, and the Muslims. It has been the playground of both the respectful and the ruthless. The Spanish coasts have been occupied by the trading empires of Carthage and Rome. All that time, Spain was told by others how to run their country, how to fight, whom to fight, and where to fight. They had one of the largest empires in the world—something history barely mentions—as they had acres of land in both North and South America, the Caribbean, Mesoamerica, and some islands in the Mediterranean. Evidence of Spanish architecture dots the world.

Yet Spain was also a battlefield for countries fighting for other causes. They were sucked into wars fought by the Carthaginians, Romans, Moors, Visigoths, British, French, Portuguese, Dutch, and Austrians, just to name a few. Some of the most famous men in history traversed Spanish soil, including Hannibal Barca, Julius Caesar, Augustus, Pompey, Hadrian, Vespasian, Trajan, Marcus Aurelius, and Napoleon. Four Roman emperors were born there, and Augustus Caesar spent his vacations there. Pablo Picasso was born in Spain, while El Greco moved there.

Many different countries and forces have had control of Spain throughout the years. Not too long ago, Spain was burdened with a dictatorship and suffered through a civil war, yet today it is an independent democracy. But how did its people do that? This book will examine the highs and lows of Spanish history and will hopefully pique your interest in learning more about it.

Chapter 1 – Prehistory

Archaeologists have found skeletal remains of early hominids in the Iberian Peninsula, which is located in the southwestern corner of Europe. These date back to the Pleistocene geological epoch when glaciers were just subsiding from the continents. It is estimated that the Pleistocene period began about thirty million years ago and ended around 11,700 years ago. The glaciers melted below the north latitude of 40°. Due to the glacial melting, sea levels rose. That, in turn, caused temporal land depressions, in which marine fossils have been found.

The earliest appearance of hominids in the Iberian Peninsula occurred during the first period of the Stone Age, that is, the Paleolithic age.

Stone Age

Around 2.5 million years ago, civilization fashioned stone tools for hunting, agriculture, cooking, and the like. Prehistoric mankind shaped these tools by striking an object repeatedly with a harder stone. The problem with stone tools is that they are crude, and it was laborious or impossible to shape them into a more useful shape. The Stone Age ended around 10,000 BCE.

Paleolithic Era

During the Paleolithic Era (the Old Stone Age), there were sub-periods/cultures that can be identified by the various tools used and the cave art. These periods, which tended to overlap, include:

The Châtelperronian

The Gravettian

The Aurignacian

The Solutrean

The Magdalenian

The Azilian

Cave art from the Châtelperronian culture has been found in the El Pendo Cave in the Cantabrian region of Spain (north-central and northeastern Spain) and depict animals they hunted. These people were hunter-gatherers who lived in communities of thirty to forty people.

The Gravettian hunting tools date back to 35,000 years ago. Tools produced during that time were tanged arrowheads, boomerangs, and blunt-backed knives.

The tools used during the Aurignacian period, which followed, include the use of bones, antlers, flint, ivory, and the like. Archaeological evidence from this period was found in the Cantabrian Mountains, which run east/west across northern Spain. The Aurignacian tools were more advanced, consisting of antler points and worked bone. The people also had flint stone tools that had notches along their blades and were more carefully hewn.

Approximately 22,000 years ago, the Solutrean culture was formed. Artifacts from that period were found in some early settlements along the northern coast of the Cantabrian Sea and the Bay of Biscay. The land of the Astures lay just toward the western areas of the Cantabrian Mountains. Many Solutrean artifacts have been found there. To the east lay the Vasco-Cantabrian region, which was peopled with the tribes of the Vascones, the Tarbelli, and the Caristiis.

Tools used during the Magdalenian period were usually small arrowheads, barbs made of flint, and chert, which was made of silica. Azilian tools were made approximately 10,000 to 12,500 years ago. They were cruder and less expensive.

Paleolithic Art

In north-central Spain, many cave paintings were found in the Cave of Altamira. They were done between 35,000 and 11,000 years ago. There are actually eighteen caves there, and the styles manifest the characteristics of the four cultures noted above: Aurignacian, Gravettian, Solutrean, and Magdalenian. Researchers also added another culture that is more specific to the Franco-Cantabrian region: the Azilian. Cave paintings from the Azilian culture have been found across northern Spain and southwestern France.

The cave art was done during the Solutrean and the Magdalenian periods. Only the mouth of the cave shows signs of human habitation, as the paintings themselves are spread throughout the length of the cave. People used charcoal and hematite, an iron ore, to create this art. The pigments were made from those materials by diluting them, and there were efforts to provide the impression of light and shadow.

The more common subjects in the paintings are an extinct species of bison—the steppe bison—horses, deer, and what looks like a wild boar. Bison representations are the most common. Images of goats were also found, along with handprints. The handprints were made by blowing pigment over one's hands to leave a negative image.

Archeologists have dated some of the paintings in the El Pendo Cave in Cantabria back to approximately 33,000 years ago during what was called the Gravettian period. Common themes were of animals that the people hunted, such as ibexes (wild goats), deer, and horses.

The El Pendo Cave was a continual Neanderthal settlement for thousands of years. It has been studied extensively by the Catalan Institute of Human Paleoecology and Social Evolution in Tarragona, Spain, along with the Institute for Prehistoric Research of the University of Cantabria. It was active between 50,000 to 60,000 years ago.

The Cave of la Clotilde in Reocín, Spain, in the Cantabrian region, has artifacts and cave paintings from the Magdalenian period between 17,000 to 12,000 years ago. The tools used then were more refined, and there was evidence the people used carbide, a mixture of carbon and some type of metallic substance. When they fashioned these tools, some of the carbide was preheated beforehand.

The Mesolithic Age

Around 10,000 BCE, the Magdalenian tools developed and began using more geometric shapes, such as triangles, and stone tools became smaller and more portable. Climatologists indicate the area was warming up. Not only were prehistoric tools found in the Cantabrian area, but they were also found farther south around Valencia and near the Mediterranean coast.

Evidence indicates that the people created semi-permanent settlements. Several villages, which held about 600 people, were found along the northern borders of the Cantabrian Sea and the Bay of Biscay. The people hunted herds of bison, wild horses, and reindeer, along with other animals, with traps, spears, nets, and snares.

Toolmaking was a commonly practiced trade. In their humble villages, there were burins (chisels), hammers, borers, wedges, barbed points, and bones that were cut in such a way as to make primitive saws. Their art manifested more naturalism. Jewelry was made, and scenes were actually painted on cave walls. Their drawings were better and showed more perspective, and there were attempts to picture things more realistically.

The Neolithic Age

The Stone Age has been subdivided into smaller segments, and one of the most important is the Neolithic Age, as significant changes occurred during that time. It is also called the New Stone Age, and it started around the 6th millennium BCE. During this time, warmer weather helped the community develop agriculture in addition to hunting to provide for themselves. This period was important because it showed a significant change in the development of civilization, specifically the introduction of agriculture. During that time, the tribes built villages instead of using temporary shelters to follow herds of wild animals.

The people had already started to grow cereal crops and ate olives. It's unknown as to whether or not they raised olive trees or ate the olives from wild trees.

Red pottery called "La Almagra" was discovered in Andalusia in southern Spain from the Neolithic era. It is made of red slip clay and is generally smooth. In several areas in southern Spain, Cardial pottery was developed. This pottery shows decorative elements, such as impressions of shells or lines and curves made with a nail or comb.

Funerary Rites

Burial rites were also established, as archaeologists have discovered dolmens. These are stone monuments consisting of two vertical stones supporting a horizontal stone, marking the sites where loved ones were buried. The remains of humans were found there, but researchers aren't sure if the remains were placed there when the people were buried. At the moment, it is impossible to date the placement of the stones with the time of the burial. Archaeologists have made the assumption that these served as markers for tombs, although there is not enough clear evidence to support this claim.

Astonishing Find!

Just recently, there was an astounding find from the Middle Neolithic period, which lasted between around 4800 to 4200 BCE. According to the Department of Prehistory and Archaeology at the University of Seville, two adult human skulls were found, one male and the other female, along with the skeleton of a young goat, in the Dehesilla Cave in Cádiz, Spain. It was a gravesite, but it was unlike other Neanderthal burial sites.

On the female's skull, there was evidence of a possible decapitation, and on the front of the skull, archaeologists found evidence of trepanation. Trepanation is a surgical technique in which a hole is drilled into the skull. One theory indicates that this may have been an attempt to alleviate a physical malady or was possibly a cure for a mental condition. An archaeological team under the direction of Daniel García-Rivero suggested that this was possibly a funerary ritual in which human sacrifice took a prominent role.

Bronze Age

The Bronze Age came later to Spain than to other countries due to the paucity of the copper needed to create bronze. In the El Argar site in southeastern Spain, bronze artifacts have been dated to around 1750 BCE. Bronze is a mixture of copper and tin. Many areas in Eurasia didn't have natural sources of tin, but the Iberian Peninsula was (and still is) rich with it. Copper, on the other hand, had to be transported from the Middle East or Indian subcontinent. Knives, spears, swords, arrow points, and large axes were all found at El Argar. The difficulties people had with bronze tools was that they broke or bent too easily.

The Tartessian culture rose in southwestern Iberia during the Bronze Age in the late 9th century BCE. Its influence spread to Extremadura in western Iberia.

Iron Age

The Greek seafarers arrived around the 9th century BCE. They used the southern coastal areas of Spain to set up trading ports near the mouth of the Ebro River, which originates in north-central Spain and flows in a southerly direction into the Mediterranean Sea. In fact, the word "Iberia" came from the Greeks. They adapted it from the Latin word "Hiberia," which was derived from the Hiberius River (now known as the Ebro River).

The Iberians were the people who dwelt in the eastern and southern coasts of the Iberian Peninsula. The term "Iberian" was generally used to refer to all the people who lived on the peninsula, regardless of their ethnicity.

In the late 8th century BCE, northeastern Iberia developed metallurgy using iron. Evidence has been found along the lower Ebro River, and it spread as far south as Castellón along the Mediterranean Sea. Greek colonies were created at Empúries along the lower eastern coast of the Mediterranean Sea.

Hominid Remains

A huge archaeological site was found in the Atapuerca Mountains, located in northern Spain, in the 20th century. Since then, its various underground levels have been continually excavated and studied. Most of the artifacts and human bones left there date to the Stone Age, but some of the levels contain artifacts from the Bronze Age.

As one might expect, the archaeological site of Atapuerca, which is today a UNESCO World Heritage Site, contains human remains. One of mankind's earliest ancestors, *Homo heidelbergensis*, was discovered there. *Homo heidelbergensis* shares characteristics of two verified ancestors of mankind: *Homo erectus* and *Homo sapiens*, today's humans. DNA evidence also showed there were bone fragments from *Homo neanderthalensis* (Neanderthals).

Many researchers have said that *Homo heidelbergensis* was a separate species, while others have argued that it evolved into *Homo neanderthalensis*. A distinct population of them evolved into Cro-Magnons and today's humans, *Homo sapiens.*

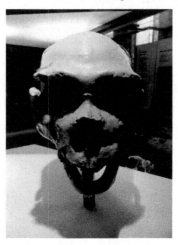

Skull of Homo heidelbergensis *found in Spain*

https://en.wikipedia.org/wiki/Homo_heidelbergensis#/media/ File:Skull,_Natural_History_Museum,_London_-_DSCF0431.JPG

The earliest Iberians were hunter-gatherers. They hunted the great wooly mammoths, saber-toothed cats, and giant sloths. These people were nomadic, as they needed to follow the animal herds.

In Escoural Cave in Montemor-o-Novo, Portugal, evidence of temporary settlements of Neanderthals was uncovered. Neanderthal remains were also found in Forbes' Quarry in Gibraltar; Zafarraya, a province of Granada, Spain; and the Cave of Salemas and the Cave of Pego do Diabo in Loures, Portugal.

The Neanderthals, who were descendants of the Cro-Magnons, gave rise to modern man. The period in which they lived may have overlapped the time when the Neanderthals existed. Evidence of this can be ascertained by the discovery of the "Lapedo child," whose mandible and cranium appear to be a hybrid between a Cro-Magnon and a Neanderthal. However, this claim has been contested, although more recent genetic work shows the possibility of the child being a hybrid.

Early Tribes

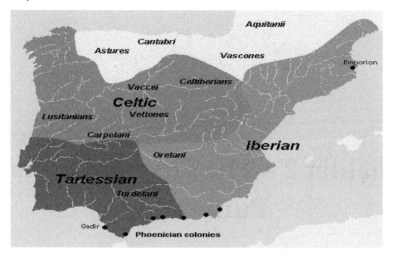

Early tribes of the Iberian Peninsula

Although it is not exactly known when the first humans arrived on the Iberian Peninsula, etymologists have studied language patterns and indicated that the Vascones, Aquitanians, Cantabrians, and Astures arrived during Paleolithic times and predate the arrival of other tribes on the Iberian Peninsula. The ancient historians, such as Titus Livius (Livy), Strabo, Gaius Plinius Secundus (Pliny the Elder), and Claudius Ptolemaeus (Ptolemy), first recorded them.

The next peoples to arrive came from eastern Eurasia, and they originated from the steppes around the Caspian Sea. They migrated westward and settled in the main area of the Iberian Peninsula. The basic tribal divisions that were noted include the Iberians, the Celts, the Lusitanians, and the Tartessians. Along the southern and eastern coasts, the Carthaginians, Phoenicians, and Greeks established settlements. Those coastal settlements were more like colonies. These civilizations used them for trading purposes, as they were all seafaring people whose homelands were elsewhere.

Chapter 2 – The First and Second Punic Wars

Prelude to War

In 270 BCE, the native people of Messana (Messina) in Sicily were occupied by the Mamertines. Hiero II, the king of the neighboring city of Syracuse on the eastern coast of Sicily, vehemently objected to that. The Mamertines felt threatened and turned to the Carthaginians and the Romans for help. Carthage responded first and established a garrison in Messana.

While the Roman Senate took some time to decide as to whether or not to intervene, Rome saw this as a golden opportunity to gain control of the Mediterranean and expand beyond Italy. As a result, Consul Appius Claudius was ordered to enter and conquer Messana in 264/263 BCE.

The First Punic War (264-241 BCE)

The word "Punic" is derived from the Latin words "poenus" and "punicus." It was intended to refer to the Carthaginians. In the course of its expansion, Carthage needed control over Sicily, an island off the western tip of Italy in the central Mediterranean. They already had established a base at Agrigento (also known as Akragas or Agrigentum) in southern Sicily.

The Battle of Messana

In 264 BCE, the Romans entered Sicily in the east and rapidly defeated Hiero II of Syracuse before going after the Carthaginians at Messana. Both infantries engaged each other, with their cavalries fighting at each end of the flanks. The Romans were disciplined soldiers and expelled the Carthaginians from the city.

Rome looked upon Sicily as a golden opportunity to expand out of Italy and gain control in the Mediterranean. In 263 BCE, Rome persuaded the independent territory of Syracuse on the eastern edge of Sicily to join them in ejecting Carthage from their base at Agrigento.

Battle of Agrigento

In 262 BCE, Carthaginian commander Hanno stationed himself outside the city along with his troops and elephants, which the Carthaginians were fond of using in battles. About twenty-five miles away from them, Roman commanders Lucius Postumius Megellus and Quintus Mamilius Vitulus were stationed with their forces. From his position, Hanno was able to cut off the supply line for the Romans encamped there. Hanno had hoped that the Romans would be defeated by their own hunger, so he waited for the Romans to leave or surrender. Six months passed, and the Roman soldiers were growing weak and ill; many were close to desertion. Hanno continued to wait.

In the meantime, the Carthaginian general Hannibal Gisco, who was inside the city with his troops, was getting desperate after the six-month siege because food for himself and his troops was running low, so he cleverly sent up smoke signals to Hanno for help.

Although there are two versions of what happened during the attack, the most likely one has to do with a cavalry and an elephant attack by Hanno in the beginning, followed by an attack on the tight Roman maniple formations of several split legions. The Romans managed to panic the elephants, which caused pandemonium, and the Romans won the battle. No doubt embarrassed by his failure, Hanno was forced to retreat.

The Romans took possession of the city and enslaved the population. Despite that, Hannibal and some of his forces escaped unharmed.

The campaign then moved to Lilybaeum in 250 BCE. In 249, while the siege of Lilybaeum was still going on, the Romans decided to attack the Carthaginians at Drepana, Sicily. The Romans dispatched a mighty fleet of their warships to surprise them. However, it was dark, and the Romans got lost. They recovered and counterattacked, but the more maneuverable Carthaginian vessels defeated them.

In 247 BCE, Hamilcar Barca, the father of the famous Hannibal, led an exhausted and limited Carthaginian land force. He fought a guerilla-style battle outside of Drepana and managed to hold on to Mount Pellegrino, a small area north of Drepana. Other land battles took place, but they were only on a small scale. Around 241 BCE, when the Carthaginians sent ships into Sicily to supply the forces still there, they were intercepted by an ungraded Roman fleet. The Carthaginians couldn't afford to add to their fleet, and Carthage ordered Hamilcar to seek a peace treaty with Rome.

The Treaty of Lutatius

By virtue of this treaty, which was signed in 241 BCE, Carthage was required to remove any remaining areas they held in Sicily. They had to release all Roman prisoners and pay an indemnity of 3,200 talents of silver.

In 237 BCE, Rome annexed the islands of Sardinia and Corsica from Carthage, while Hamilcar Barca was engaged in a mutinous mercenary rebellion. That was in contravention of the treaty, as Carthage had occupied those islands since the 6th century.

When Carthage attempted to recover the islands of Corsica and Sardinia, Rome considered it an act of war.

The First Punic War was a terrible loss for Carthage, but in a sense, it was a moral loss for Rome. After witnessing the cruelty of the First Punic War, the people of Sicily and other non-Romans were angry and bitter against Rome.

It led the ancient historian Polybius to write, "There is no witness so dreadful, no accuser to terrible, as the conscience that dwells in the heart of every man."

Barcid Spain

After losing their base in Sicily, Hamilcar Barca sought permission from the Carthaginian Senate to recruit a new army. Because the predominant influence in the Senate at the time was Carthage's anti-war faction, which was led by the very conservative Hanno II the Great, there was little objection to maintaining a defensive force.

Once Hamilcar assembled a military force, he deliberately didn't seek any further advice from the pacifist Carthaginian Senate. Instead, he boldly took his forces across the western Mediterranean in 237 BCE. They landed at Gades (Cádiz) on the southwestern coast of the Iberian Peninsula. Hamilcar was anxious to prevent Rome from getting a foothold on all the coastal colonies around the sea. If Carthage had possessions in Iberia, that might help make up for the losses of the First Punic War. The only sea trading colonies that Carthage had in Spain at that time were Gades, Abdera, Malaca, and Sexi.

Hamilcar brought his son-in-law, Hasdrubal the Fair, and his son, Hannibal, along with him. Hamilcar realized that Rome had every intention of subjecting all the nations along the northern Mediterranean, which would cripple Carthage. On one occasion, he took his young son aside and had him make a pledge: "I swear as soon as age will permit, I will use fire and steel to arrest the destiny of Rome."

Next, Hamilcar secured the aid of the Tartessian tribes in order to gain access to the gold and silver mines of Sierra Morena. However, he also needed the cooperation of the Turdetani or Turduli tribe, who dwelled near the foothills of the Sierra Morena. The areas there were occupied by the Celtiberians, and they objected to this intrusion. Hamilcar and his mercenary forces attacked the tribe. Hamilcar won the battle and crucified the Celtiberian commander, but he let 10,000 of the others return home.

Once Hamilcar had control over the mines, he could pay for Iberian mercenaries, which would allow him to secure more control over Iberia. Hamilcar also secured access to the Guadalquiver and Guadalete Rivers in order to set up a mining operation. Once he streamlined the process, Hamilcar was able to send silver back to Carthage to pay off the war debts.

In 236 BCE, he sent Hasdrubal back to North Africa to conduct some campaigns for Carthage. While there, he amassed mercenary soldiers from Numidia and other African regions to take back to Iberia.

In the meantime, Hamilcar traveled eastward toward Cape Nao on the northeastern coast of Iberia and was met with resistance from some Iberian tribes, as well as a smaller tribe, the Bastetani, but overcame them. In 235 BCE, he founded a settlement called Akra Leuke, meaning "White Mountain." Today, it is known as Alicante. He used Akra Leuke to guard the Carthaginian holdings in southern Iberia.

When Rome heard that Hamilcar was in Iberia, they sent him an inquiry as to his motivations. Fortunately, Hamilcar was able to elude their attention by simply responding that he was raising money to pay off Carthage's war debts.

On his way through Iberia, Hamilcar waged war with the troublesome Oretani tribe. There are multiple theories about the subsequent occurrences. One theory indicates that during the ensuing conflict, the Oretanis sent burning ox carts toward his position. Once the fiery carts crossed the Jucar River, the oxen panicked. Hamilcar was caught up in the melee and died in the chaos. In another version, which was related by the ancient historian Appian, Hamilcar fell from his horse and drowned.

The recorded date for Hamilcar's death was 228 BCE. Carthage had lost one of its most powerful leaders.

The Ebro Treaty

Rome was concerned about Carthage's continued presence in Iberia. Therefore, in 226 BCE, Hamilcar Barca's son-in-law, Hasdrubal the Fair, signed a treaty with Rome, which stated that neither nation would cross the Ebro River. This river runs from northern Spain and into the western Mediterranean Sea. However, this treaty wouldn't last long for too long, as Hannibal was about to enter the picture in a big way.

Battle of Saguntum

In 220 BCE, the city of Saguntum, a Roman ally, was engaged in a civil war. Rome intervened and brought peace to the city. The Roman leaders then advised the city leaders to execute anyone there who supported Carthage's presence on the Iberian Peninsula. The city leaders did so. However, they also, on occasion, attacked neighboring tribes who had good relations with Carthage. Hannibal wanted revenge for that, but he also wanted to prevent Rome from extending its interests to the rest of Iberia. He mainly wanted to prevent Rome from gaining more control over the Mediterranean Sea trade. Hannibal sought the permission of the Carthaginian Senate to annex Saguntum (today's Sagunto). In addition, Saguntum lay south of the Ebro River, so traveling there wouldn't be a violation of the Ebro Treaty.

Historians estimate that Hannibal set out with 20,000 to 40,000 troops and 40 elephants into southern Iberia. It was said that he financed part of his planned journey with silver from the mines just outside the Carthaginian city of Qart Hadasht (which would later become New Carthage). In 219 BCE, Hannibal Barca captured and secured control of Saguntum on the southern coast of Iberia. Rome demanded that Carthage hand over Hannibal to them and withdraw from Saguntum. Carthage refused, kicking off the Second Punic War.

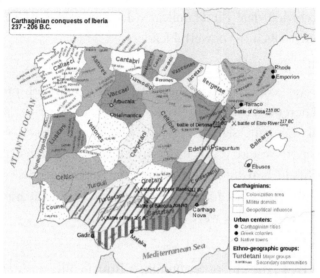

Carthaginian Conquests in Iberia, 237-206 BCE

https://upload.wikimedia.org/wikipedia/commons/4/49/Iberia_237-206BC.svg

Historians' Argument: Then and Now

Both ancient and contemporary historians have argued about whether or not Hannibal had broken the Ebro Treaty by going north of the Ebro River. Although the map shows that this was clearly not the case, ancient writers like Appian blamed Hannibal for triggering the Second Punic War by crossing the river. Other ancient historians, like Polybius, posed other reasons, but he also mistakenly added that Hannibal had broken the Ebro Treaty, which was untrue.

Many historians—both ancient and contemporary—added to the confusion. For example, Livy, who was known to editorialize, indicated that Hannibal actually said, "It was I who first began that war [the Second Punic War] against the Roman people."

However, it was Rome who crossed the Ebro River when they intervened in Saguntum when it was engaged in a civil war. No doubt, Hannibal also remembered the pledge he had made to his father, the one where he would "arrest the destiny of Rome."

The Second Punic War (218-201 BCE)

The Second Punic War was fought on several fronts, including Iberia, Italy, and North Africa. It was also called the "War against Hannibal," that bold and notorious Carthaginian commander and son of Hamilcar Barca.

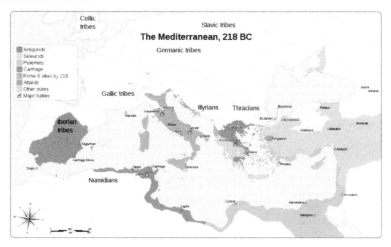

Tribal Regions during the Punic Wars

https://en.wikipedia.org/wiki/Battle_of_Insubria#/media/
File:Mediterranean_at_218_BC-en.svg

Obsessed with keeping his pledge to his father by destroying Rome, Hannibal boldly marched his troops and elephants through Iberia and Gaul (France) and then over the massive Alps. Men and animals fell just trying to negotiate the treacherous mountain passes in the severe cold of the craggy heights. According to Polybius, 20,000 men perished and most of his elephants. This left about 26,000 men left to fight.

Hannibal spent much of his time in Italy after this point, so his story in Spain ends here. However, the Punic Wars continued to be fought on Spanish soil. Hasdrubal Barca, the younger brother of the famous Hannibal, was in charge of protecting Carthaginian interests along the Ebro River while Hannibal marched toward Italy.

Carthaginian Campaign in Iberia

The Battle of Cissa

In the fall of 218 BCE, the Roman general Gnaeus Cornelius Scipio Calvus landed on the southern Iberian coast at Emporiae (Empúries). The Carthaginian commander Hanno and his Iberian mercenary forces then marched toward the town of Cissa, located on the southeastern coast of Iberia. He had a force of about 11,000 men. The Romans, on the other hand, had twice that number. At the Battle of Cissa, Hanno was captured and lost 8,000 men, with 2,000 of them being taken as prisoners. In addition, Indibilis, the chieftain of the Ilergetes, a small Iberian tribe, was captured along with some of the tribal members. The Romans raided Cissa but were disappointed, as there were little valuables to loot.

The Battle of the Ebro River

In the spring of 217 BCE, Gnaeus Scipio mobilized the Roman navy, taking fifty-five ships to the mouth of the Ebro River in southern Iberia. Hasdrubal Barca ordered Himilco, a Carthaginian leader, to ready their fleet. When the word came, though, Himilco's men had been ashore foraging. Although they rushed back, it was too late. As soon as the Carthaginian ships exited the mouth of the river, the awaiting Romans sunk four of their vessels and captured two more. Many of the Carthaginians beached their ships and fled. The Romans then towed away twenty-five of the Carthaginians' abandoned ships. The Battle of the Ebro River was a horrendous loss for Carthage.

The Battle of Dertosa

In the spring of 215 BCE, Hasdrubal Barca led the Carthaginian army into the Battle of Dertosa (also known as the Battle of Ibera), in present-day Tortosa, Spain. Hasdrubal went up against two powerful generals, Gnaeus Scipio and his brother Publius Cornelius Scipio.

Although the sizes of their forces are unknown, they are estimated to have been around 25,000 each.

Hasdrubal put his unarmored Iberian infantry in the center of the battlefield and his heavily armored troops on the left. His Numidian light cavalry was at the right side of the flank, and his heavier Iberian and Libyan cavalry were on the left. A skirmish line was in front with his elephants.

The Romans used their traditional formation of two legions in the center with Italian forces to either side. Their skirmish line was out front, and its men were armed with javelins.

The Carthaginian cavalry attacked the Romans' flanks, but it still had to do battle with the legions, which rushed forth at them. The Iberians fled from the oncoming onslaught. The Romans then circled around the rear of the Carthaginians, who were now basically surrounded. Hasdrubal and most of the cavalry were able to flee, along with the elephants. The Romans nearly annihilated the Carthaginians who were left behind on the battlefield. It was a disaster for the Carthaginians.

The Battle of the Upper Baetis

This area was the scene of a double battle, that of Castulo and Ilorca. In 212 BCE, Publius and Gnaeus Scipio hired 20,000 Celtiberians to supplement their Roman forces, which had been reduced in the battles with the Carthaginians. Hasdrubal Barca and his brother Mago, along with Hasdrubal Gisco, divided the Carthaginian army into two divisions, which included some allied Iberian forces as well. Publius Scipio attacked Mago at Castulo in south-central Iberia, and Gnaeus Scipio clashed with Hasdrubal Barca at Ilorca to the west.

The Battle of Castulo

Mago Barca and Hasdrubal Gisco held back, instead sending in the Numidian cavalry to harass the Roman troops of Publius Scipio. Publius and his troops dealt with the Numidians and then went after

Mago's Iberian allies, who were about to encircle his army. However, the Romans were weakened because they had lost a lot of men to the Numidians. When Hasdrubal Gisco and Mago arrived on the scene, there wasn't much the Romans could do. Many fell on the battlefield that day, including Publius Scipio. It was an incredible victory for the Carthaginians.

The Battle of Ilorca

Prior to the major attack, Hasdrubal Barca and his men had convinced many of Rome's mercenaries not to fight, and they deserted the field. When Gnaeus Scipio was preparing for the attack at Ilorca, he saw the Carthaginian forces racing toward him, which included not just Hasdrubal Barca but also Hasdrubal Gisco and Mago. Because he had already lost many of his warriors to desertion, Gnaeus Scipio tried to withdraw to the north. He was forced to flee to a hilltop, where he tried to dig in. However, the ground was too rocky for digging defensive walls, so they set up their saddles and baggage as a defensive shield. The Carthaginians routed them with ease. Gnaeus Scipio was killed, along with many Roman soldiers as well.

The surviving Romans then headed north of the Ebro River. There were only around 9,000 at that time, which was less than half of their initial number.

The Carthaginians were pleased with their victories at Ilorca and Castulo, and they let the remnants of the Roman army go. That was a dangerous mistake.

Roman Reinforcements Coming!

The year was now 211 BCE. The Carthaginians were benefiting from having conquered nearly half of the Iberian Peninsula. However, some of the Roman survivors who had escaped from the Battles of Castulo and Ilorca contacted Gaius Claudius Nero, the chief Roman general (not to be confused with the emperor of the same name). After the survivors told Nero about their losses in Iberia, he dispatched 13,000 more Roman soldiers to the peninsula. Nero put them under the command of Publius Scipio's son, the more famous Publius (Publius Cornelius Scipio Africanus).

The Romans readied themselves for an attack on the capital of Barcid Spain: Qart Hadasht.

The Siege and Fall of New Carthage

In 209 BCE, Carthage's main seaport of Qart Hadasht, of which they were so proud, was blockaded by a Roman fleet of thirty-five warships. The city was surrounded on three sides by water, so the Carthaginians were basically blocked in. When the Romans arrived, led by Gaius Laelius and Publius Scipio Africanus, the Carthaginian army was ten days away, so the citizen militia had to fend for itself until help arrived. Rome particularly wanted to cut off the financing of Hannibal's march through Italy, as he was getting the silver he needed to pay his soldiers and supplies from Qart Hadasht. Two thousand men slipped out of the city gate to hold off the Romans in their camp to the east and prevent them from using their siege engines to mount the city walls. The Carthaginians were very skilled and fought hard and long against the Roman soldiers. But Scipio had been anticipating such a move, and he forced the Carthaginians to flee back to the city.

Laelius's fleet sailed to the southern side, but the Carthaginians beat them back. Scipio pulled back, but he renewed the assault later in the day. Unfortunately for the Carthaginians, a squall blew through the area, nearly emptying the lagoon to the north. Aided by this twist of fate, the Roman soldiers under Scipio waded through the lagoon, mounted the north wall, and entered the city with ease. The Romans had been ordered to kill everyone they met. Polybius summed up the scene by saying, "One can see...not only humans who have been slaughtered, but even dogs sliced in two and the limbs of other animals cut off."

After taking control of Qart Hadasht, Scipio changed the name of the city to Carthago Nova ("New Carthage").

The Battle of Baecula

In 208 BCE, the Roman commanders had been ordered to stop Hasdrubal Barca, who was on his way through southern Iberia to join his brother, Hannibal, in Italy. At the time, the Carthaginians had about 30,000 men. The Roman commanders, Scipio Africanus and Gaius Laelius, had 30,000 Roman warriors and 10,000 mercenaries.

Hasdrubal spotted the Roman troops and moved to a double-tiered plateau south of the town of Baecula in south-central Iberia. He posted his light troops on the lower level with his main entrenchment behind. There was a valley there, and Scipio dispatched a Roman unit to block the entrance to it so the Carthaginians wouldn't be able to retreat. He also hid his main unit to deceive the Carthaginians. The Romans sent up a volley of arrows and rocks and moved upward toward the Carthaginians. Once the Romans in the front had mounted the incline, Hasdrubal Barca sent out his light troops to attack. Despite their disadvantage, Scipio and his men were able to repel them with ease.

Following that, Gaius Laelius led the heavy Roman forces forward to the right of the enemy, while Scipio hit the left flank. Since Hasdrubal couldn't see the hidden Roman forces, he didn't believe he was dealing with a major conflict, so he didn't properly deploy his men. Once the forces were engaged in hand-to-hand combat, Scipio's hidden unit sprang out and hit Hasdrubal's men. The Romans then slashed at the Carthaginians from three sides.

Once Hasdrubal realized he'd been trapped, he found a way to break through, and he retreated in secret with a smaller force. Even though he tried, Scipio failed to stop his Roman legions from raiding the Carthaginian camp, which delayed him from pursuing Hasdrubal.

The Battle of Ilipa

Hasdrubal Barca had departed Iberia to join up with his brother, Hannibal, in Italy, but he was killed at the Battle of the Metaurus in 207 BCE. Mago Barca and his co-commander, Hasdrubal Gisco, then recruited Celtiberian mercenaries from the central regions of the peninsula. In the spring of 206 BCE, they marched eastward. They had around 54,000 to 74,000 troops and 32 elephants.

Scipio Africanus had approximately 48,000 to 55,000 men, and he sent his troops faster than the Carthaginians. His light troops and cavalry attacked the edges of the Carthaginian flanks. He also attacked the Carthaginian wings, which made it difficult for the Carthaginians to form another sensible defensive formation. Once the Romans had obliterated the Carthaginian forces at the wings, the Carthaginian forces in the center were thrown into confusion when the maddened elephants rushed forward. In the chaos, many Iberian mercenaries deserted.

The Carthaginians, hungry and weary, tried to retreat to their camp. Although they made it back, Scipio ordered a full-scale assault. The remnants that were left fled up a mountain, with the Romans at their heels. When the Romans caught up with them, the butchery commenced.

Mago Barca managed to slip away in the bedlam and headed east along the southern coast of Iberia. He then detoured toward the Balearic Islands in the Mediterranean, where he planned to cross into Italy to help Hannibal. Hasdrubal Gisco left for his home in Carthage. But because he had been unsuccessful, Hasdrubal Gisco was attacked by a mob of angry Carthaginians in 202, and he committed suicide in order to escape their wrath. Livy described him as "the best and most distinguished general this war produced after the three sons of Hamilcar." The Roman consul at the time, Quintus Fabius Maximus Verrucosus, however, insulted his memory by saying that Gisco "showed his speed chiefly in retreat."

After the Battle of Ilipa, about 48,500 Carthaginians had been either killed or captured. Although this wasn't the end of the Second Punic War, it was the end of the conflict in Spain, as the Carthaginians were ejected from Iberia.

Chapter 3 – Rome Entrenching

After the Second Punic War, Publius Scipio Africanus returned from Rome's successful campaign in Africa. He made allies of the various Iberian tribes, agreeing to offer them protection. Ever conscious about defense, the Romans set up permanent garrisons at the key cities of Tarraco (Tarragona) on the southern shore, Carthago Nova (Cartagena) in southeastern Spain, and Gades (Cádiz) on the southwest coast. Scipio insisted that the tribes who had fought against them as mercenaries for Carthage pay tribute, which consisted of clothing, supplies, and food for Roman soldiers who were stationed there. Sardinia and Sicily, which had been ceded to Rome after the Second Punic War, were required to provide the Romans with grain. There were fertile valleys along the Ebro River, and the farmers there produced vegetables for the Romans.

In 218 BCE, Iberia was divided into two provinces: Hispania Citerior ("Nearer Iberia") and Hispania Ulterior ("Further Iberia"). They were named due to their distance from Rome; Hispania Citerior was closer to Rome, while Hispania Ulterior was farther away. Over time, more provinces would be added, which included Hispania Lusitania, no doubt after the tribe who inhabited it, the Lusitanians; Hispania Baetica, which was named after the Bastetani people who inhabited parts of that region there; and Hispania Tarraconensis, after the town of Tarraco in northeastern Hispania.

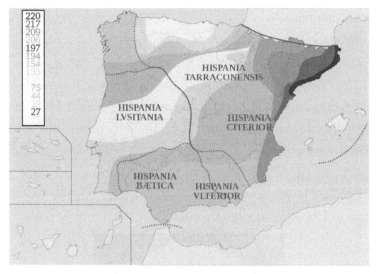

Provinces of Rome by 14 BCE

*https://en.wikipedia.org/wiki/Roman_conquest_of_the_
Iberian_Peninsula#/media/File:Conquista_Hispania.svg*

In 206 BCE, two men, Lucius Cornelius Lentulus and Lucius Manlius Acidinus, were sent to Hispania with powers similar to governors, although they didn't hold the official power of a Roman praetor, which was customary. A praetor was a magistrate who held nearly as much power as a Roman consul, which was the highest office in Rome. The men that were called upon to act as praetors were inexperienced but greedy. They often abused the people and took advantage of their distance from the Roman Senate. In the year 199 BCE, Lentulus and Acidinus were replaced by Gnaeus Cornelius Blasio and Lucius Titus Stertinius; this time around, the two men were praetors.

Things were not always peaceful while Rome established its control. Each province was supported by Roman infantry and cavalry, who were kept occupied by regional wars. In 198 BCE, two Lusitanian chieftains rebelled: Luxinius and Culchas. Just two years later, Hispanic tribes under Budares and Baesadines revolted, and as many as 12,000 Hispanics were slaughtered in the ensuing conflict.

Cato's Campaign

In 197 BCE, Cato became the praetor of Hispania Citerior, and he ruled with an iron fist. One of his sayings was, "War feeds upon itself." Cato used that as a rationale for passing harsh penalties when they were called for. Although he claimed he "pacified Hispania," his actions induced more rebellions. Thus, his own saying, that war feeds upon itself, came true.

Marcus Porcius Cato, who later became a Roman senator, was a military man. He was a strict and exacting leader, and he was sent to Hispania in 195 BCE to calm the rebellions.

Cato the Elder

https://en.wikipedia.org/wiki/Cato_the_Elder#/media/File:Patrizio_Torlonia.jpg

Cato disembarked with his troops at the town of Emporiae, on the border of Hispania and Gaul. He was fierce in his battles, and he was also skilled at bribery and exploitation. Sometimes when fighting broke out in Hispania, he offered to pay the Celtiberians to help him with his campaign. According to ancient biographer Plutarch, when

Cato's officers complained that he was paying the "barbarians," he said, "There was nothing terrible in it; should they be victorious, they could pay the price with the spoils taken from the enemy, not out of their own purse." He went on to explain that there would be no record of this payment since it wasn't taken from the Roman treasury.

Cato was a hard-working man who shared his food with his soldiers and worked alongside them. However, he was very much in charge. He planned everything very carefully and coordinated his activities with others. But though he was practical and realistic, he was not a man of compassion. His life was a celebration of the cult of self-aggrandizement.

When Cato became concerned that the tribes north of the Ebro River were becoming restless, he disarmed them all. The Bergistani tribe complained about this, and he leveled the walls of their cities. Once he saw Cato in action, Publius Manilus asked for his help in dealing with the battle preparations of the Turdetani mercenaries. Cato presented them with three options: 1) to return to their homes, 2) to receive double their pay from the Romans, or 3) to set a date for battle. When the mercenaries didn't respond, Cato plundered their lands.

When trouble broke out among other tribes in the Ebro River Basin, Cato captured several towns as a demonstration of his power. After that, the Ausetani, Sedetani, and Suessetani tribes swore their allegiance to him. When a neighboring tribe, the Lancetani, failed to do the same, Cato attacked and subdued them. Whenever a tribe didn't follow his orders, there was always retribution.

The First Celtiberian War (181-179 BCE)

There were six tribal nations who were identified as Celtiberians due to the similarity of their language and appearance. They lived in Hispania Ulterior and Citerior. The tribes were called the Belli, the Arevaci, the Lusones, the Titti, the Vaccaei, and the Pellendones. Praetors Quintus Fulvius Flaccus and Publius Manlius were in charge, and the territory over which they ruled was extended to include some of the neighboring regions for the sake of bringing peace to Iberia.

In 181 BCE, the Celtiberians rebelled against Roman rule. They gathered up an army of 35,000 men and positioned themselves in the central area of Carpetania in the southern regions of Iberia. Flaccus drew up 6,000 infantrymen, who were allies from friendly tribes, along with 3,000 regular Roman soldiers and 300 cavalrymen. Flaccus had his brother, Marcus Fulvius, collect two squads of soldiers and encamp nearby. With his combined army, he defeated the Celtiberians and occupied their town of Aebura.

The Celtiberian forces then moved to Contrebia. However, when they arrived, they saw that the Romans had already occupied it, but the Celtiberians believed they had moved on, so they took no precautions. The Romans suddenly emerged from the city gates and surprised the Celtiberians. The two armies clashed, and as many as 12,000 tribal members were slaughtered. Afterward, the Romans ravaged the countryside.

In 180 BCE, the Romans were reorganizing, and Flaccus was headed for Tarragona on the southeastern coast. The Celtiberians set a trap for him at the Manlian Pass in the mountains. Once Flaccus and his soldiers entered the pass, the Celtiberians leaped upon them from two sides. The Romans drew up their usual tight formation, and the enemy went into a wedge formation to jam them in. With their tight formation, the Romans were able to throw the tribal warriors into disarray. It was a heavy loss for the Celtiberians, who lost 17,000 men.

To aid in the war effort, commanders Tiberius Gracchus and Lucius Postumius Albinus were in charge of maintaining order in Hispania Citerior, and they activated their forces on their side of the border in 179 BCE. Albinus went to the land of the Vaccaei, farther north and east of Celtiberia. Albinus reported that he conquered and killed 35,000 of them.

Gracchus went to the town of Munda and defeated them in a night attack. He took hostages and left a garrison of soldiers behind. While moving on to the town of Certima, he burned the countryside. There, Gracchus was met with messengers from the town, who asked how Gracchus planned on conquering them. Gracchus then showed the envoys the size of his forces. When they saw the size and strength of the Roman forces, the townspeople surrendered without a fight. They were required to pay an indemnity and gave the Romans some of their young nobles to fight alongside them after taking an oath of loyalty to Rome.

Gracchus then moved on to Alce. Here, he planned a feint attack. He sent out his native mercenaries, who pretended to be overwhelmed by the Alce fighters. After seeing that, the Alce soldiers were filled with overconfidence and fiercely attacked. Suddenly, Romans leaped out from behind the ramparts and routed the Alce men, killing 9,000 and taking 320 as prisoners.

In a plundering rampage, Gracchus and his men forced the Celtiberians of 103 towns to submit. Filled with revenge, he returned to Alce and besieged the city. They initially resisted, but when Gracchus employed his siege engines, the people retreated to their citadel and then sent out messengers to offer their surrender. Gracchus accepted the daughter and two sons of the city's powerful chieftain, Thurru, as hostages. Following that, Thurru himself approached Gracchus and asked that his family be spared. Gracchus agreed, and from that point on, Thurru served as a Roman mercenary.

The Second Celtiberian War (154-151 BCE)

By the time the Second Celtiberian War broke out, the Celtiberians had formed a confederacy among their various subtribes, including the Pellendones, the Lusones, the Titti, the Belli, and the Arevaci. Rome was annoyed that the Belli had started building walls around its city of Segeda, and Rome declared war. The Romans intensely disliked any show of resistance, as they felt they were far more superior and needed to keep the tribes subservient.

An Argument about a Wall!

Around 153 BCE, the Belli indicated that they had agreed to the terms laid down by Gracchus and that he hadn't forbidden the construction of a wall around their city of Segeda. The headstrong senators back in Rome disagreed about the construction of the wall and were insulted that they hadn't given special permission for this. The Romans also didn't trust that the Belli would remain peaceful.

The Titti, the Belli, and the Arevaci agreed to participate in the war until arrangements for a peaceful co-existence could be made. However, his rambunctious co-commander, Quintus Fulvius Nobilior, preferred a total and complete surrender.

After seeing these developments, the Belli sought refuge among the Arevaci. The Arevaci even tried to mediate with Nobilior, but it was fruitless. Thus, a courageous Segedan townsman by the name of Carus volunteered to fight. He took 20,000 men and battled with Nobilior and his troops. Nobilior was defeated, but he scored a major victory—the courageous Carus was dead. There were roughly six thousand dead on both sides.

The Arevaci next went to the town of Numantia, where they chose Leuco and Ambo as their leaders. Nobilior raced over there with some Numidian mercenaries and elephants. When the combined Celtiberian forces spotted the huge elephants, they panicked, as they'd never seen elephants before. Thus, the Celtiberians rushed back behind their city walls. A fierce and bloody battle ensued. When a stone hit an elephant squarely on his head, the poor animal went berserk, causing the other elephants to do so as well. As a result, they trampled the Romans!

Marcus Claudius Marcellus replaced Nobilior in 152 BCE. The Arevaci, Titti, and Belli sued for peace. The Roman Senate refused, though, and started gathering troops to send to Hispania. They also appointed Lucius Licinius Lucullus as the new Roman consul in 151 BCE and sent him to replace Marcellus once his term expired. Before that happened, Marcellus really wanted to create a peace arrangement with the tribes. He made a deal through the intercession of Litenno, the Numantine leader. The tribes then handed over the required hostages and sent money to guarantee their promise.

Lucullus's Illegal War

The ambitious Lucullus soon arrived. Instead of leaving matters as they were, he was anxious for fame and stirred up the people, first demonstrating his prowess by attacking the Vaccaei, a peaceful tribe.

He then provoked the Caucaei. When they asked for terms of peace, Lucullus took tribute and had his men kill the adult males in their town of Cauca (today's Coca). Only a few of the inhabitants escaped alive. When reproached for this by the people of Itercatia, Lucullus became furious and laid waste their fields.

Lucullus then went to Pallantia and sent his men out to forage for food. The locals harassed the Romans, making it impossible for Lucullus to get supplies, including the gold and silver he had heard these people possessed. Lucullus was constantly pursued by the Pallantians and other Celtiberians. They chased him and his men north to the Douro River and out of their territory.

The Lusitanians: Terrors of Rome!

When the Carthaginians controlled Hispania, they didn't occupy the whole Iberian Peninsula. However, the arrival of the Romans was a shock for many Hispanic tribes. One such tribe was the Lusitanians in western Hispania.

The Lusitanian War started during the Second Celtiberian War in 155 BCE. It was triggered when Punicus, the chief of the Lusitanians, attacked some of the lands nearby that belonged to Roman subjects. With this move, Punicus gained the support of the Vettones and the Blastophoenicians. However, Punicus was soon killed in a raid. He was succeeded by Caesarus, who continued to rebel against the

Roman occupiers. The Treaty of Atilius was signed in 152 BCE, but war erupted again when Lucius Licinius Lucullus, who had fought in the Second Celtiberian War, provoked the Lusitanians.

In 150 BCE, the Roman praetor of the region, Servius Galba, pretended to pacify them, giving them each plots of land on which to farm. In exchange, he promised peace and told them to lay down their arms.

Appian reported that he "told them as friends to lay down their arms." However, when they did so, "he surrounded them with a ditch and sent in soldiers with swords who slew them all. Thus he avenged treachery with treachery in a manner unworthy of a Roman, but imitating barbarians."

Viriathus, the scourge of Rome

In 148 BCE, the Lusitanians ambushed the Roman soldiers at Tribola. The Lusitanians lost the battle, but a hardy warrior named Viriathus escaped. The Romans received reinforcements, but they, too, were all slain by Viriathus and his men.

In 142 BCE, Fabius Maximus Servilianus then took charge of the Roman legions and marched against Viriathus. Maximus had a tremendous force of 18,000 infantry and 1,600 cavalrymen. Viriathus wasn't able to defeat Maximus, but he and his men were able to inflict 3,000 casualties, but he had to constantly defend himself until the Romans moved on to Itucca. Maximus recaptured some of the cities Viriathus had occupied. It was said that Maximus captured as many as 10,000 men and beheaded 500 of them. The rest were sold into slavery.

In the town of Erisana, Viriathus asked for a peace treaty. The treaty was broken by Rome upon the arrival of Maximus's replacement: Fabius Maximus Caepius. Caepius took over Viriathus's annexed town of Arsa, but Viriathus cleverly escaped. To retaliate, Caepius attacked the neighboring Vettones and Callaici, destroying their crops.

Viriathus still wanted peace, so, in 140 BCE, he sent envoys to the new consul, Quintus Servilius Caepio, to draw up terms. Caepio, though, bribed Viriathus's envoys and had them assassinate Viriathus.

The assassination of Viriathus

https://en.wikipedia.org/wiki/Lusitanian_War#/media/
File:Madrazo_Viriatus_HighRes.jpg

Tautalus replaced Viriathus as the chief of the tribe. He lacked the tactical skills that Viriathus had, and he knew it. Nevertheless, he knew his people counted on him to be honorable and pick up the gauntlet from his illustrious predecessor.

Tautalus took Viriathus's remaining loyal forces and attacked the Roman allies at Saguntum, where he was defeated. From there, he and his men marched to Hispania Ulterior and was confronted with the formidable Roman legions of Caepio at the Baetis River. Tautalus was defeated and surrendered. Caepio gave them lands in southern Iberia, possibly around the city of Valencia.

The Numantine War

The Numantines were a subdivision of the Lusitanians who lived by the Douro River. The Numantines defeated two great Roman generals: Consul Quintus Caecilius Metellus Macedonicus and Quintus Pompeius. Pompeius, it seems, was a very ineffective Roman soldier. He lost a number of battles to the Numantines, so to avoid future hostilities with the tribe, he negotiated a secret treaty with them. However, the treaty never truly came to fruition, as Marcus Pompillius Laenas soon came to assist in the war effort. When the Numantines returned to complete their obligations under the treaty, Pompeius denied that any treaty existed at all. They sent in Gaius Hostilius Mancinus to subjugate the Numantines. The tough Numantines assaulted Mancinus, and they defeated him until he was forced to accept a treaty. Rome wasn't satisfied and handed over Mancinus to the Numantines to be their prisoner.

In 134 BCE, Rome sent in Consul Scipio Aemilianus to resolve the issue to their liking. He brought a huge army with him, which consisted of 20,000 men and 40,000 allies. Once he arrived at Numantia, he built a ring of seven fortresses around the city. After that, he created a dam out of a nearby swamp, and a lake formed. He had his archers mounted on towers ten feet off the ground, allowing them to easily besiege the city with volley after volley of arrows. Scipio also lowered the Douro River and strung sharp blades across it to prevent anyone from escaping. The Numantines were effectively trapped.

Their leader, Rhetogenes, managed to get out despite the blockade and went to a neighboring region, Lutia, begging for help. The young men from Lutia responded positively, but the more wary Lutian leaders told Scipio about it. In retaliation, Scipio went after the youths and cut off their hands! Such was the cruelty rendered to the people in Iberia.

Numantia sent out ambassadors, offering complete surrender in exchange for freedom. Scipio adamantly refused. He wanted vengeance. When the Numantian envoys returned with the bad news, the incredulous people murdered them for their failure and vehemently refused to surrender.

It was truly the most tragic of tales. When the people started starving, they engaged in cannibalism. Others committed suicide. Eventually, the Romans set fire to the city to force them out. The ancient historian Appian related that, when those who still lived emerged, they came out "looking altogether inhuman, with their bodies unwashed, full of hair and nails and filth; they smelt horribly and their clothing was unwashed and just as stinking...they looked at the Romans in a way which expressed their pride and grief." That tragic year was 133 BCE.

Ruins from the siege of Numantia

Rome Turns Its Attention Elsewhere

Rome tasked the praetors with securing and maintaining peace in the Hispanic provinces. Although the main rebellions—those of the Celtiberians, Lusitanians, and Numantines—were over, the revolts hadn't ended, but they were more sporadic and local. Many may have been resurgences of tribal hostilities that existed prior to the Roman conquest, and others were caused by the restrictions mandated upon the people.

Rome was in the process of building an empire in Western Europe, as well as in Hispania. The Cimbric War, which was fought from 113 to 101 BCE, took place mostly in central Europe, but some of it spilled over into northern Hispania when a Germanic tribe, the Teutons, invaded there. The Celtiberians also involved themselves in the war by crossing the Hispanic borders and fighting against the Teutons and other Germanic tribes.

As for the people of Hispania, the ancient biographer and historian Plutarch commented upon what he saw in the state of Hispania Ulterior. "The province was still uncivilized in its customs and in a savage state, and robbery was at that time still considered a most honorable occupation."

Chapter 4 – Roman Hispania

Caesar's Civil War

Prior to the time when Rome called itself an empire, Rome's government was known as the Roman Republic. The Romans had divided themselves into two political factions: the Optimates ("best ones") and the Populares ("favoring the people"). The Optimates were conservatives who basically favored the upper classes, as they believed they were the most qualified to run governmental affairs. The Populares were average citizens who felt that Rome and its colonies should be run by the people through its assemblies.

In 60 BCE, the First Triumvirate was established. This was an alliance between three notable politicians: Marcus Licinius Crassus, Gnaeus Pompeius Magnus (better known as Pompey), and Julius Caesar. After the death of Crassus in 53 BCE, the Triumvirate ended, as Caesar and Pompey were at odds with each other.

In 50 BCE, Caesar and Pompey warred with each other over control of Rome and its territories. Caesar was broadly supported by the Populares, while Pompey was supported by the Optimates.

The Crossing of the Rubicon

Rome had a law that governors and promagistrates had *imperium*, meaning "right to command," but only within the Roman provinces outside of Italy. There, they could march at the head of the army. *Imperium* was held by the elected magistrates and consuls of Italy alone. Governors and generals from other provinces could not march into Rome at the head of an army; their armies had to be disbanded beforehand. It was considered a capital offense not to do so.

The Rubicon River marked the northern border of Italy, and Caesar wanted to march his army into Rome in triumph. He was, after all, the governor of Cisalpine Gaul and had conquered the rest of Gaul in his earlier campaigns.

The ancient historian Suetonius indicated Caesar hesitated before boldly crossing the Rubicon, saying the immortal words, "The die has been cast." The date was January 10th, 49 BCE.

Pompey and his supporters fled Rome, including Titus Labienus, Caesar's former lieutenant. Labienus changed his allegiance to Pompey after Caesar crossed the Rubicon, as did Publius Attius Varus, who went back to his former post in Africa. Caesar, along with Mark Antony, pursued Pompey into Dyrrhachium across the Adriatic Sea and into Illyricum (today's Albania).

The Battle of Dyrrhachium

In July 48 BCE, Pompey's troops outnumbered those of Caesar. Pompey and his men managed to blockade Caesar, placing him in a terrible position. However, when his faithful friend, Mark Antony, counterattacked, it looked like Caesar was going to be successful. Due to Antony's skillful tactics, Pompey's forces became disorganized. Caesar had his right flank stand firm until it was clear they were horribly outnumbered and then ordered a retreat. Caesar lost between 1,000 to 4,000 men, and Pompey lost over 2,000.

The Battle of Pharsalus

In August 48 BCE, at Pharsalus in central Greece, Titus Labienus had his cavalry attack Caesar's cavalry at his left flank, pushing them back. However, Caesar had men hidden, and they suddenly raced forward. Pompey's cavalry panicked, and Caesar's men chased after them while they ran for the hills. The left wing of Pompey's forces remained, but they had no backup. So, Caesar's left wing swung around and went after them, and his third line of troops under Mark Antony assaulted the remainder of Pompey's men head-on. It was brutal, and all Pompey could do was retire from the battlefield and leave his troops in the center and the right to continue for as long as they could hold out.

Caesar had his men raid Pompey's camp. Pompey's auxiliaries in the camp defended it as best they could, but they couldn't last for long. Labienus fled to Corcyra, a Greek island. Pompey took his family, his gold, and cloak and went to Egypt.

Caesar left his legate, Quintus Cassius Longinus, in charge of Hispania and headed to other fronts that were more important in the context of the war, like Greece and Egypt. In September of 48 BCE, Pompey was assassinated in Egypt on Pharaoh Ptolemy XIII's orders. He thought it would gain Caesar's favor, but when Pompey's head was brought to Caesar, he was horrified. Some have wondered if he didn't manipulate the circumstances that led to Pompey's death, but most agree Caesar likely wouldn't have wanted Pompey to suffer such an inglorious insult by being beheaded.

During that time, Caesar increased the size of the Senate, so it could represent more people. He also regulated the distribution of grain, supported military veterans, reformed the tax codes, granted citizenship to people in Rome's many provinces, and even worked on creating the Julian calendar.

The Battle of Munda

In March 45 BCE, Caesar returned to Hispania and fought the Battle of Munda in southern Hispania Ulterior against Gnaeus Pompeius (also known as Pompey the Younger), the son of Pompey. Pompeius was joined by Titus Labienus and Publius Attius Varus.

The battlefield was on a slightly sloped hill. Caesar unsuccessfully tried to lure the Optimates down. Since that maneuver failed, he instead made a full-frontal assault. Caesar took command of his right wing and fought off the Pompeian right wing, weakening it. Pompeius had his generals dispatch some men from their left flank to strengthen his weak wing. That was a mistake, as Caesar then sent in his cavalry to attack the Pompeian rear. Labienus moved in some troops to intercept them, but the men in the center mistook that for a retreat. Labienus and Varus were both killed. The Pompeian forces broke up, and there was bedlam. Many fled to the city of Munda and were killed.

The Pompeian forces went on the run, pursued by Caesar and his men. Pompey's son was wounded and had to be carried on a litter near the lines of battle. He and his forces then took shelter near the town of Lauro.

The Battle of Lauro

At the Battle of Lauro, which was fought in early April of 45 BCE, some of the local people informed Caesar of the whereabouts of the Pompeian soldiers. Caesar's soldiers then surrounded them. The Pompeians were aided by uneven terrain, which allowed them to keep up their defensive attacks. The fighting was brutal, and the Pompeians incurred heavy casualties. Pompeius hid in a cave, but the locals informed Caesar of this, and they hunted him down. Caesar had him executed, and Pompeius's head was severed from his body and displayed to the local people.

In 44 BCE, Julius Caesar was assassinated in Rome by his political rivals who feared his power. After all, he was declared dictator in perpetuity only a month before his death. He was succeeded by his adopted son, Octavian, who became the first emperor of Rome in 27 BCE.

The Cantabrian and Asturian Wars (29-19 BCE)

Throughout the early history of Hispania, there were troublesome tribes in the north. Among them were the Cantabrians and the Astures. Both of these tribes were from Celtic stock. They had spent the early times of Roman expansion in the Iberian Peninsula as mercenaries. During the Punic Wars, they fought on the side of the Carthaginians.

The ancient Roman historian Florus once wrote, "In the west almost all Spain had been subjugated except that part which adjoins the cliffs where the Pyrenees end and is washed by the nearer waters of the ocean." That was the land of the Cantabrian and Asturian tribes.

The Cantabrians and Astures were formidable enemies. When all was said and done, eight Roman legions had been sent to fight them, which numbered between 70,000 and 80,000 men.

In 29 BCE, the great Roman general Titus Statilius Taurus was sent to subdue those northern tribes. In 28 and 27 BCE, Sextus Appuleius II took over. When his term of duty was over, Appuleius returned to Rome and was celebrated in triumph.

In 27 BCE, Augustus made his debut as the commander of the ongoing war. Before going to Hispania, Augustus checked on the conditions in Gaul. He didn't reach Hispania until later in the year, reaching Tarraco (Tarragona) right before winter arrived. In 26 BCE, Augustus actually began to fight, setting up a three-pronged attack.

The first division attacked the Celtiberians at the city walls of Vellica, where they routed them. The enemy fled to Mount Vindius in the Cantabrian Mountains. Augustus's second division marched to

Aracelium and wiped out the town. The third division went to Gallaecia in northwestern Hispania. The Cantabrians made their last stand at Mount Medullus. Augustus's soldiers dug a fifteen-mile ditch and put the area under siege. The Cantabrians knew that the Romans would either slaughter them or capture and sell them into slavery. They wanted to avoid that, preferring suicide to slavery. According to Florus, they vied with one another to hasten their deaths "in the midst of a banquet by fire and the sword and a poison which is there commonly extracted from the yew-tree." Many committed suicide rather than capitulate to the Romans. However, some preferred to live, and they surrendered to Augustus in person in 25 BCE.

The war was not over, though, for the Astures were not ready to capitulate. In 25 BCE, the Astures were encamped in the mountains, and they came down the slopes in droves. The Astures broke up their forces into three divisions to attack the Romans from their three encampments. The Astures' position and attack plans were betrayed by one of their subtribes, and Publius Carisius, who was in command of the Roman legions, was able to attack them by surprise.

Carisius attacked the Astures mercilessly. They resisted, but in the end, they were unable to repel the Romans. The Astures then fled to the fortified city of Lancia. Lancia permitted the Astures entry, but the Romans threatened to burn the city. The Asturian general begged mercy for his soldiers, indicating that Lancia would be a better monument to a Roman victory if left untouched. The Romans acceded and withdrew, knowing that they had won a psychological victory.

The war would continue on and off until 19 BCE, but the victory was already Augustus's by this point, and he annexed all of the Iberian Peninsula. Although minor rebellions would still occur, Augustus felt he had successfully pacified Hispania, and he made it his objective to introduce the region to the riches of Roman culture and society.

Pacification and Development

Even during the times when Rome suppressed the rebellions of the Hispanic tribes, its ultimate motivation was pacification and assimilation. Gradually, the Romans sent in their war veterans to work and populate the lands.

Miraculous Aqueduct at Augusta Emerita

https://en.wikipedia.org/wiki/Acueducto_de_los_Milagros#/media/ File:El_acueducto_de_Los_Milagros.jpg

Augusta Emerita

The Romans established Augusta Emerita (today's Mérida, Spain) in central Hispania in 25 BCE. It was the capital of the province of Lusitania. Since they wanted to inculcate their settlers and the people of Hispania with Roman history, they built the Provincial Forum there in the 1st century CE. It had an adjoining temple to the goddess Diana. In addition, the Romans also erected a circus for chariot races. It could hold as many as 30,000 people.

Augusta Emerita was beautiful, but it was subject to droughts. Therefore, the Romans realized they had to build an aqueduct to supply the city and crops with water. This was called the *Acueducto de los Milagros* ("Miraculous Aqueduct"). It carried fresh water from the Proserpina Dam in Extremadura. Another dam, the Cornalvo Dam, was also constructed in Extremadura and is still being used today.

Asturica Augusta

In 14 BCE, the Romans established a city in the current province of León, in northwestern Hispania. Today, the city is called Astorga, and its name is derived from the Roman city, which they called Asturica, after the Astures, who lived there. During Roman times, the city provided an essential thoroughfare for the transport of copper from the mines of Rio Tinto in southwestern Hispania and silver from Emerita (Mérida).

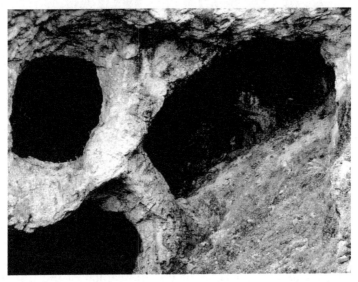

Roman copper mine near the Rio Tinto River

Tarraco

Tarraco, modern-day Tarragona, was the oldest Roman town in the Iberian Peninsula, and it was the capital of Hispania Citerior in the 1st century BCE. The ancient writer Pomponius Mela described Tarraco as "the richest port on this coast." Located on the southeastern coast of Hispania on the Mediterranean Sea, Tarraco stands as a majestic memorial of the past.

The Arch of Berà in Tarragona (Tarraco)

https://en.wikipedia.org/wiki/Arc_de_Ber%C3%A0#/media/
File:Spain.Catalonia.Roda.de.Bara.Arc.Bera.jpg

Under Caesar Augustus, the city flourished. He used Tarraco as a place to rest when in poor health. It was a bright sunny city, and when he was ill or during the winter months when he wasn't directing battles, he went there to rest.

Augustus rebuilt a road that had been originally put in by the Carthaginians and rerouted it to go from Narbo Martius (Narbonne) all the way to Gades (Cádiz) near the tip of southern Hispania. This was called the Via Augusta, and it was completed after Augustus's death in 14 CE.

During Augustus's reign, the city had an amphitheater and a provincial forum. Romans used slaves for gladiator combat in the amphitheaters. However, if soldiers lost battles, they were sometimes condemned to fight to the death in the arena. Romans could lose their status as free men for debt and petty crimes, and they, too, were forced into the arenas. Other gladiators volunteered for it, as gladiatorial combat could make a strong man very wealthy.

Today, Tarraco is one of the largest archaeological sites in Spain and is a World Heritage Site.

Baelo Claudia

Located just near the tip of Hispania and Gibraltar, this town was very wealthy, as it was able to benefit from the commerce on the Mediterranean Sea and the eastern Atlantic Ocean. The height of its importance was reached during the 2nd century CE, but it fell into disuse because of a number of earthquakes in the several centuries that followed.

The city was noted for its tuna fishing. In Baelo Claudia, "garum" was made. This was a fermented fish sauce with a savory taste. It was popular not only in Rome but also in the previous Hispanic colonies of the Phoenicians. It was manufactured in various grades, and the top residue, which was called *allec*, was spooned off and given to the poor to flavor their farina, which was a type of flour they used for their food.

Panorama of Baelo Claudia

https://en.wikipedia.org/wiki/Baelo_Claudia#/media/
File:Baelo_Teatro_panorama.jpg

Although it seems pedestrian, garum was a popular product and a major export. In time, it became a staple in Roman cuisine. Garum was also modified to make liquamen, which was also quite nutritious.

The Romans used it to feed their soldiers. Since one of the ingredients was sea salt, it acted as an effective preservative for fish. Sometimes, it was used for medicinal purposes.

Roman Bridges

Many of the rivers in Hispania were wide, so the Romans built grand stone bridges over the major rivers. These bridges were attractive; many arches were used for support, and the pillars in the water at each end of the arches were heavily reinforced.

The ancient Romans used segmental arches in the construction of the supports for the bridges. The segmental arch was less than 180°. It added more height to the lower portion to compensate for flooding. Other bridges had larger arches, like the one pictured below. They were quite beautiful, and many still stand today as a testament to the architectural skills of the ancient Romans.

The Alcántara Bridge in Extremadura

https://en.wikipedia.org/wiki/Roman_bridge#/media/File:Bridge_Alcantara.JPG

Caesaraugusta

Caesaraugusta, today known as Zaragoza, located in northeastern Hispania, had been populated by the Sedetani tribe. The Romans founded a city there for the war veterans from the Cantabrian Wars. It is not known when exactly it was founded, but it is believed to have been built between 25 and 11 BCE.

The Romans built a magnificent theater nearby. Greek and Roman plays were performed there, mostly tragedies and comedies. Roman comedies depended upon stock characters, one or more of whom would be the protagonist in the play:

the *adulescens* - a single man in his late teens

the *leno* - a character who was immoral

the *senex* - a parent concerned with his relationship with his son, who gets involved in poor or illicit relationships

the *parasitus* –a nuisance, as the term implies

the *miles gloriosus* - an arrogant character, a braggart

the *virgo* - an innocent young maiden

the *matrona* - the mother or wife who interferes with her children's lives

Amphitheater at Caesaraugusta

The amphitheaters were also used for civic celebrations, which were intended to impress the Hispanic population with Roman sophistication and power. It was considered a sign of status if a town had its own amphitheater.

Romanization of Hispania

The architects of Hispania themselves started to design their own towns after the Roman style. They built public buildings and even bathhouses for their own people. After a community would do this, the Romans awarded the town with the status of *municipium*, which gave the people of the city the "Latin right," meaning they had extra privileges. Those practices accelerated under the reigns of Emperors Vespasian (69-79 CE), Titus (79- 81 CE), Domitian (81-96 CE), and Hadrian (117-138 CE).

Vespasian extended the privileges of the Latin right to all the communities of Hispania, although there were some who didn't conform, like a community near Seville, where archaeologists discovered bronze tablets with orders issued by Emperor Domitian for the people to conform to the Roman customs and laws.

Most of the privileges the native (Hispanic) communities received most likely only applied to the elites of the districts, as no mention was made of the lower classes.

When the uprisings later decreased, the number of Roman legions serving in Hispania was gradually reduced. By Vespasian's reign, there was only one Roman legion left, and it served in today's province of León.

Religion

The Roman deities started to be assimilated into the pagan belief system of the early Hispanics. In Gades (Cádiz), a blend of Hercules, the great Roman god, and Melqart, the Phoenician goddess of the sea, was manifested in a cult built up around the two.

In the 1st century, Christianity began taking root in Hispania. In 286 CE, Diocletian split the empire into two sectors: the Eastern Roman Empire and the Western Roman Empire. During the reigns of Diocletian and Maximian, as well as Galerius and Constantius Chlorus, who followed, edicts were passed that required Christians to obey traditional Roman statutes. Those laws stated that people were to return to the worship of the Roman gods.

Constantine I, also known as Constantine the Great, became the emperor in 306, and he would later go on to reunite the Roman Empire. In 313 CE, he legalized the Christian religion, and on his deathbed in 337, he became the first Roman emperor to convert to Christianity.

Chapter 5 – Enter the Germanic Tribes and the Muslims

During the early 5th century, the Visigoths, a Germanic tribe, migrated westward through Europe. When the Roman Empire was invaded by the Vandals, Alans, and Suebi, Rome asked King Wallia of the Visigoths for military assistance. The Visigoths were then made *foederati* of Rome, meaning that this assistance would result in benefits for the Visigoths.

The Fall of the Roman Empire

In 409 CE, the Vandals crossed the Pyrenees and started settling in Hispania. Two of their sub-tribes, the Hasdingi and Silingi, settled in Hispania after receiving land grants from Rome in exchange for their military assistance. At this point, Rome started losing control of Hispania.

The Suebi tribes under King Rechiarius invaded Hispania. By 432, the Suebi had ravaged Hispania and controlled most of the peninsula.

In 456, King Theodoric II of the Visigoths defeated Rechiarius near Astorga in northwestern Hispania. His troops then sacked several Suebi towns and massacred many people. After that,

Theodoric took over Hispania Baetica in the southwest and part of Hispania Lusitania.

In 466, Euric rose to the Visigothic throne. He attempted to consolidate the Iberian Peninsula. He took the rest of Hispania Lusitania and captured Hispania Tarraconensis by 472.

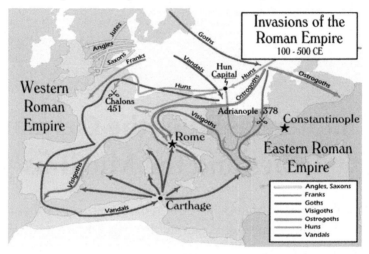

Roman Empire circa 500 CE

https://en.wikipedia.org/wiki/Roman_Empire#/media/
File:Invasions_of_the_Roman_Empire_1.png

Two years later, Julius Nepos became the de facto Western Roman emperor. In 475, he was usurped by Orestes, the top military commander of the Roman forces. Orestes then crowned his sixteen-year-old son, Romulus Augustus, the next emperor of Rome. His *foederati* demanded they be given a third of the land in Italy. Orestes refused, and when they rose up against him, Orestes fled. The tribes had appointed an officer named Odoacer as their king, who chased down Orestes and killed him. The sixteen-year-old Romulus was dragged before Odoacer, where he surrendered his throne. Odoacer looked down upon the boy, and in a compassionate gesture, he allowed Romulus to settle in Campania in Italy. According to the legend, what became the great Roman Empire was founded by a boy named Romulus. In 476, it was ended by a boy named Romulus.

Romulus Augustulus surrendering to the Germanic chieftain Odoacer

https://upload.wikimedia.org/wikipedia/commons/6/68/
Young_Folks%27_History_of_Rome_illus420.png

Visigothic Rule

The Visigoths then controlled all of Iberia. In around 589, the Visigoths converted to Christianity. In 654, the Visigothic king, Recceswinth, published a law code named *Liber Iudiciorum*, also known as the Visigothic Code. Prior to this code, Iberia had different laws for Romans and Visigoths, but King Recceswinth eliminated these legal and social distinctions. *Liber Iudiciorum* united various aspects of the tribal codes, Catholic law, and Roman law.

The Visigoths placed their capital in the Kingdom of Toledo. In 574, the Visigothic king, Liuvigild, fought against the Cantabrians and established the Duchy of Cantabria. In 578, King Liuvigild built the city of Reccopolis in central Iberia, doing so in the Byzantine style of eastern Europe. It contained a grand palace, a mine, and a church.

Basilica and grounds at Reccopolis
https://en.wikipedia.org/wiki/Visigothic_Kingdom#/media/
File:Recopolis_-_Basilica_(Exterior).jpg

One of the areas that were left unmolested by the Romans was the land of the Basques. They lived in the upper northeastern area of Iberia in the mountains of the Pyrenees. Up until then, the land of the Basques was used as a crossroads for Europe. The Visigoths, though, wanted to conquer and control them. For over two centuries, the Basques and the Visigoths fought battle after battle. Those attacks tended to make the Basques unite more closely, and they fought to preserve their language, *Euskara*, and their culture. In fact, the Basques even held on to their old nature religion for many years.

During this time, education spread throughout Iberia, led by scholars such as Bishop Isidore of Seville, an expert in etymology; Eugenius I of Toledo, who was skilled in mathematics and astronomy; Theodulf of Orléans, a poet and theologian; and King Sisebut of the Visigoths, who was a poet.

Goldsmiths of the Visigothic Era

In times past, the term "Visigoths" was associated with barbarianism. However, the art and jewelry of the Visigoths show a great deal of artistry and professional skill. Two of the most prized pieces from that era are votive crowns. They are made of gold and interspersed with precious stones, such as sapphires and pearls, among others.

Eagle-shaped brooches called fibulae demonstrate the delicate work performed by master goldsmiths. These were found in necropolises belonging to noble families.

Symbols of military rank were visible in a soldier's belt buckle, and they were imitations of the Byzantine style. They were decorated with lapis lazuli, a semi-precious stone.

The Visigothic architecture in their churches followed the traditional cruciform pattern, and some churches were built upon the foundations of old Roman buildings, like the Church of Santa María de Melque, for example. Later on, the Knights Templar, one of the organizations that aided in the Crusades, cleverly converted the dome of the church into a turret for defensive purposes. Horseshoe-shaped arches were developed by Visigothic artisans, and they supported the vault under the overhead apse.

Religion

Contrary to popular opinion, the Visigoths were Christians. However, they followed Arianism, which promoted the doctrine that Jesus Christ is a distinct entity from God the Father and is subordinate to Him. This strand of Christianity was promoted by Arius, a presbyter in Alexandria. Catholicism rejected that belief as heresy. Many Visigoths later converted to Catholicism. There was some friction between the Visigoths and the Catholics in Iberia, but those conversions helped ease the tension between them.

Umayyad Conquest

The Muslim Umayyad Caliphate (661–750) engaged in conquests like the caliphates before it, incorporating North Africa, among other areas. In 710, Musa bin Nusayr, the ruler of Muslim North Africa, dispatched Tariq ibn Ziyad to raid Iberia. He took mostly Berbers along with him, although there were some Arab warriors as well.

The Berbers were from North Africa (namely Morocco, Tunisia, and Algeria), and they were Islamic converts. The non-Muslim community called them the "Moors," named after the country of Mauretania, in northwestern Africa, where they came from. In time, the Moors came to represent Muslim inhabitants in the Iberian Peninsula and elsewhere in Europe.

The Battle of Guadalete

Tariq sailed for Gibraltar and confronted the troops of King Roderick of the Visigoths, who was returning from an engagement with the Basques. The two armies met at Guadalete, which is thought to have been near Cádiz, on the western shore of Iberia. Although the numbers of warriors participating may not be accurate, primary sources state that Roderick had 100,000 warriors and Tariq had 187,000. The Visigoths engaged in a number of very violent hit-and-run raids, never attacking with full force. That gave the Muslims an opening, and King Roderick was slain early in the battle. It was a brutal, bloody battle. The Visigothic casualties were not recorded, while one chronicler estimates the Muslims suffered 3,000 dead. More contemporary historians indicate that treachery had caused Roderick to lose control. The defeat of the Visigothic army essentially left Iberia open for invasion.

After the rule of the Visigoths, the assimilation of the Visigoths and Hispano-Romans occurred at a fast pace. The nobility thought of themselves as the "Hispani" or the "gens Gothorum" and thought of themselves as one people. Some of them fled to Asturias or Septimania.

In the mountain areas of the Cantabrian and Pyrenees Mountains, the Cantabrians, Astures, Basques, and the people from western Galicia remained unassimilated. The territories around the Pyrenees, in particular, continued to resist assimilation into the cultures of their conquerors.

The Muslims generally left the non-Muslims alone to practice their own religion, but they did treat them as second-class citizens, insisting that they pay a special tax called the jizya.

In 713, Abd al-Aziz ibn Musa took control of the territory occupied by the Visigothic governor Theodemir, who was living in southeastern Iberia with his followers. The Muslims permitted him to establish an autonomous kingdom there, but it functioned as a client state, and they, too, paid the jizya.

In 714, the Muslim commander Musa Ibn Nusayr marched up the Ebro River to take on the western Basque territories and the tribes in the Cantabrian Mountains. It was reported he had little or no opposition in these regions. However, the far northern areas weren't their main focus, as the mountains were steep and inhospitable. The Muslims managed to reach the city of Pamplona in 714. The Basques in that city submitted after hammering out a compromise with the invaders.

Internal Conflicts between the Moors and Arab Factions

When Arab Muslims settled in parts of Iberia, there were ethnic tensions between them and the Moors from North Africa. The Arab Muslims attempted to place the jizya on them, and rebellions broke out, first in North Africa and then in Iberia. In 740, the inhabitants gave up their garrisons in León, Astorga, and other northwestern territories.

In 750, the Umayyad dynasty was overthrown by the Abbasids. However, the Umayyads would not sit still for too long. In 756, Abd al-Rahman I, a prince from the deposed Umayyad dynasty, seized power in Córdoba, establishing the Emirate of Córdoba. This allowed Muslim power in al-Andalus to stabilize. In 778, he campaigned in Zaragoza in northeastern Iberia and gained a measure of control there. He also gained control of Pamplona and the Basque lands in 781.

The aristocrats of al-Andalus embraced Islam in order to maintain power, but the majority of the population were Christians.

In the 10th century, al-Rahman's descendant, Abd al-Rahman III, declared that he alone was the caliph of Córdoba and severed all loyalties to the Syrian and Egyptian caliphates. He was more interested in maintaining his power base in North Africa, but he was unable to do so and remained isolated from the Muslim world.

Death in the Name of Religion

Abu Amir Muhammad ibn Abdullah ibn Abi Amir al-Ma'afiri, better known as Almanzor, became the chancellor of the Caliphate of Córdoba in the 10th century. He was essentially the ruler of Iberia, as the caliph was young, inexperienced, and weak, but Almanzor never ruled in name. Almanzor made it his objective to see that all of Iberia recognize his sovereignty. In 977, he started conducting military campaigns, which became more frequent and violent as he gained more power. Although they disagree as to the details, historians estimate that he conducted assaults on Christian areas in Iberia about fifty-six times, killing and slashing Christians as he raged through the country. That generated a state of insecurity, and Christians took refuge in fortified towns and castles. Almanzor mercilessly plundered the Christian areas, but he didn't occupy the areas he assaulted. Thus, most people returned when he left, which prevented long-term ruin.

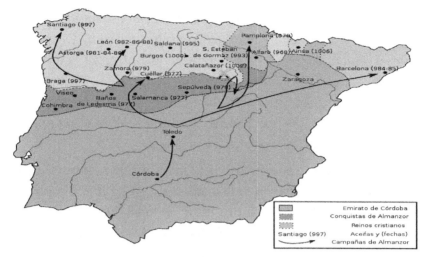

In 985, Almanzor sacked the city of Barcelona. In 988 and 989, he and his troops assaulted Zamora, Toro, Astorga, and León in northwestern Iberia.

Military campaigns of Almanzor

https://en.wikipedia.org/wiki/Almanzor#/media/File:Map_Almanzor_campaigns-es.svg

As noted in the map, the Muslims essentially had control of nearly all of Hispania, with the exception of the northern areas. Those continued to be controlled by the Christians.

Battle of Religions

In 929, the Caliphate of Córdoba fell apart. The former caliphate was broken up into taifas, which were independent entities in the Iberian Peninsula. The leaders of these principalities often raided Christian lands and carried Christians away to serve as slaves. The taifas then started fighting with each other, becoming weaker as a result.

The Siege of Toledo

In 1085, the Christian king Alfonso VI of León and Castile found an opportunity to expand his lands when Yahya al-Qadir became the new leader of the Taifa of Toledo. He wanted Alfonso's help in putting down an uprising, but instead of that, Alfonso took Toledo for himself. Alfonso agreed to award al-Qadir the control of Valencia. Al-Qadir accepted, but some of the local people objected. Throughout the years, Alfonso continued to expand his territories while ensuring his control remained strong. In 1099, Alfonso took back Valencia with the help of El Cid. During this time, Alfonso repopulated Salamanca, Segovia, and Ávila with Christians.

The taifas grew concerned when the Christians started gaining territory in Hispania. They called upon the Almohad Caliphate, a Berber Muslim empire in North Africa, to help. The founder of the Almohads, Ibn Tumart, was a Muslim scholar. His was a school of Islam that adopted what was called the "Ash'ari" school. It ascribes to Sunni Islam, but it contains a mixture of other beliefs as well. The Ash'ari school maintains a very orthodox approach to Islam and still exists today.

Battle of Alarcos

The Almohads, under Abu Yusuf Ya'qub al-Mansur, fought for control of the province of Castile in 1195 against King Alfonso VIII of Castile. Alfonso underestimated the strength of the Muslim forces. During the battle, Alfonso's cavalry became disordered, and they were almost completely surrounded and were virtually destroyed as a result. Castile then lost control of the area, and nearby castles were surrendered or abandoned.

The battle against the Muslims in Iberia took on a religious significance. The papacy justified war against the Muslim invaders, saying it was in defense of Christianity, as they considered the Muslims to be "infidels." Christian groups called "orders" were founded to combat this threat, such as the Order of Santiago, the Order of Calatrava, the Order of Montesa, the Order of Alcántara, and the Knights Templar.

The Battle of Las Navas de Tolosa

This battle took place in July 1212 in southern Iberia. Alfonso VIII of Castile was aided by soldiers from the Christian Kingdom of Navarre, which was led by Sancho VII, and King Peter II of Aragon. They surprised the Almohads at their camp and raided it. According to legend, during the attack, they came upon the tent of the caliph himself, Muhammad al-Nasir. The caliph escaped, but many Muslims were slain. Christian domination was secured after this battle.

Repossession of Spain

While the Muslims were trying to hold on to the southern areas of Spain, the Spanish provinces in the north were being integrated into Christian territories. They then started using the word "Spain," taken from the Castilian word *España*, to refer to themselves and again reestablished their provincial borders.

The Kingdom of Asturias was willed to Fruela II in 910 after the death of his father, Alfonso III. The Kingdom of Asturias transitioned into the Kingdom of León in 924 when Fruela II became the king of León.

Around 1230, the Kingdom of León and the Kingdom of Castile were merged when Ferdinand III of Castile was bequeathed the Kingdom of León. This laid the foundation for the Crown of Castile, which was a polity that combined the two powerful territories.

The Kingdom of Navarre had been stabilized and was ruled by Sancho VII in the early 13th century.

The Kingdom of Aragon was led by King James I in the early 13th century. Remnants of the Almohad warriors from the campaigns of Almanzor occupied the Balearic Islands, off the coast of Spain. James and Spanish allies from Catalonia took troops to the island of Majorca to expel the Muslims. In 1229, they tried to reconquer Majorca but didn't succeed until 1231.

By 1250, the taifas were in decline, and the repopulation of the Christians started in the northern Douro River Valley in central Spain, part of the Ebro River Valley running from northeastern Spain diagonally into the Mediterranean, and the central segment of Catalonia in the eastern area. The southern area below the Douro River was resettled by Christians during the following two centuries.

The *Fueros*

A *fuero*, or "charter," was a set of laws and privileges that was usually regionally based and was intended for a certain group of people. For some regions, it had the weight of a constitution. The term was first used during the Middle Ages and referred to the body of regulations and rewards or easements granted by a monarch. In exchange, the peasants agreed to defend the land for the monarch or church official in the case of church property.

As peasants returned to the land, they claimed areas that were suitable for farming. Once that occurred, the population of the provinces grew, and commerce abounded.

The establishment of the *fueros* laid the foundation for modern Spain's autonomous communities.

The Last Muslim Holdout

The final holdout for Muslim power in Spain was the Emirate of Granada in the far south. It lasted well into the 15th century, dissolving in 1492. By then, the dawn of Habsburg Spain was just on the horizon.

Chapter 6 –The Transformation of Spain

The 14th and 15th centuries proved to be a pivotal period in Spain. It marked the critical difference between what was and what was to come.

The Battle of Vega de Pagana

The Battle of Vega de Pagana was fought in 1339. It was the battle for the conquest of Granada, the last Muslim stronghold in Spain. It pitted King Alfonso XI of Castile with his Order of Alcantara against Abu Malik, the son of the sultan of Morocco, Abu al-Hasan Ali, and his troops. Abu Malik's father had kept the peace signed in 1334, but he wanted to expand.

Historians have little details as to the logistics of the battle, but Abu Malik was killed.

Battle of Río Salado and the Spanish/Muslim Campaign at Gibraltar

In late 1340, Abu al-Hasan, the sultan of Morocco, receive an appeal from Sultan Yusuf I of Granada to help drive out the Castilians. The Muslims assembled their fleet under the command of Muhammad ibn Ali al-Azafi.

The Castilian fleet met the Muslims at the Castilian outpost of Gibraltar, where they were met by forty-four galleys under the command of Admiral Alfonso Jofre de Tenorio. Al-Azafi surrounded them, and Tenorio was killed.

Thinking that it would take the Castilians a long time to rebuild their fleet, Abu Hasan placed a siege on Tarifa near Cádiz. Believing he had time, Abu Hasan sent some of al-Azafi's galleys back, leaving only twelve for himself.

Alfonso XI sought the aid of the king of Aragon and King Afonso IV of Portugal. In addition, they swiftly constructed extra ships at Seville and moved them in place to block any supply lines to the Muslims. With 20,000 Castilian, Aragonese, and Portuguese on their way, Abu Hasan lifted the siege and moved up on a hill between Tarifa and the sea. Yusuf I, Sultan of Granada, placed his forces on a hill nearby. During the night, Alfonso XI reinforced his garrison at Tarifa, meeting only slight resistance from a light Muslim cavalry. Abu Hasan's Muslim scouts either failed to see that the city was being reinforced or were afraid of admitting it. This would be a serious mistake.

King Alfonso XI, who led the main force of Castilian fighters, decided he would attack Abu Hasan's main troops, while Afonso IV of Portugal would take on Yusuf's Granada forces. The Orders of Alcántara and Calatrava bolstered up the Portuguese. After much effort, the Spanish forces aided the vanguard troops in crossing the Salado River.

Afonso ordered a full-scale attack with just himself and his troops. However, the rearguard arrived on the scene just in time to help, attacking the Muslim forces from the rear. The Muslims broke rank and fled toward the city of Algeciras. The entire battle took just three hours.

The Muslims ran to the Guadamecí River, and the Spanish pursued them. There, the Spanish raided their camp, even taking hostages and prisoners, included females. Some of the sultan's wives were even killed.

Siege of Algeciras

Algeciras was just a short bay away from the tip of Gibraltar. The Muslims had been routed from their strongholds north of there during the Battles of Vega de Pagano and Río Salado. The survivors had retreated to the fortifications at Algeciras.

Alfonso XI placed a siege upon the Algeciras Muslim stronghold in 1342, and he received side from Juan Núñez III de Lara and a number of other Spanish fighters. Alfonso divided their forces between three men: Don Juan Manuel, Pedro Fernández de Castro, and Juan Núñez himself. After nearly two years, the Muslims finally surrendered.

The Fifth Siege of Gibraltar

As one might expect by the name, this was the fifth time the Spanish and the Muslims fought over Gibraltar in a span of forty years. They staged a long siege and dug defensive ditches all around it, as well as across the isthmus to blockade the Muslims from accessing supplies and reinforcements.

The siege continued on during the fall and winter, but there was still no indication that the garrison would surrender. Suddenly, the Black Death hit. It infiltrated the Castilian camp, and many died. However, Alfonso was determined and hung on. Then King Alfonso himself was struck with the plague. He died on Good Friday, March 26th, 1350. His forces notified Yusuf I, the sultan of Granada, who was commanding the Muslim forces there. He courteously permitted the Spanish soldiers to leave as they carried the body of their deceased king.

Peter of Castile

In 1350, Alfonso XI was succeeded by his son, Peter. Peter was then declared Peter I, King of Castile and León. Peter's mother was Maria of Portugal. He was under the firm hand of his mother until he was encouraged to free himself from her influence by the powerful noble Juan Alfonso de Albuquerque.

Peter was a good-looking young man, and it is said that he secretly married lovely María de Padilla, who was being raised in Albuquerque's household. She convinced Peter to rid himself of Albuquerque's influence, placing him back under the influence of his mother and the other nobles. Not knowing of his marriage to María, Peter's mother and the court nobles convinced Peter to marry Blanche of Bourbon in 1353.

Peter deserted Blanche but pursued his relationship with María, with whom he had had four children.

The War of the Two Peters and the Castilian Civil War

This war, as one might have guessed, involved two Peters: Peter I, King of Castile, and Peter IV, King of Aragon. Peter of Aragon supported the accession of Henry of Trastámara, who was the illegitimate son of Alfonso XI and his mistress, Eleanor de Guzmán. Peter of Castile, on the other hand, was the legitimate son of Alfonso XI.

In 1357, the Castilians conquered Tarazona in Aragon, which was followed by a temporary truce. In 1361, the war broke out again. Queen Blanche had been imprisoned so she could be out of the way for Peter to enjoy his other dalliances, but Peter still seemed to see her as a threat. Although it is not known for certain, some believe Peter had her executed. This is just one of the reasons why Peter was called "Peter the Cruel" by his contemporaries.

The fighting between the two Peters resumed. The Castilians captured the fortresses at Verdejo, Alhama, and Torrijos, among other places. However, a new peace was soon arranged, and all those conquered forts were returned to their owners.

In the following year, Peter of Castile called upon Charles II of Navarre, Edward III of England, and Edward's son, who was known as Edward the Black Prince. Peter of Castile then caught Peter of Aragon off guard and conquered Arize, Atece, Terrer, Moros, Cetina, and Alhama. After this, Peter of Castile went back to Seville.

The hostilities continued, and in 1366, Henry Trastámara, who was in France, gathered a large army of Aragonese nobles and English mercenaries. He had the support of the kings of both Aragon and France, Peter IV and Charles V, respectively. With this alliance, Henry invaded Castile, causing Peter to flee.

Peter of Castile did not want to go out without a fight, and he called upon his supporter, the Black Prince, for aid, promising the prince some lands in Castile. The Black Prince was pleased with this arrangement and brought along some English mercenaries with him.

At the Battle of Nájera in 1367, Edward the Black Prince restored Peter to the throne. However, Peter didn't keep his promise and never paid Edward for his service. Edward's health was poor, and he soon left the Iberian Peninsula.

That was the signal for Henry Trastámara to return. In 1368, he did so, and the Cortes of Burgos recognized him as the king of Castile. Peter, though, did have some supporters, and eventually, there was nothing left to do but decide who the ruler would be on the battlefield. In 1369, the Battle of Montiel was waged. Their forces confronted each other, and Peter was ultimately slain.

Death of "Peter the Cruel"

Henry Trastámara then became Henry II, King of Castile in 1369.

The Fernandine Wars and Treaty of Salvaterra

After the death of Peter of Castile and the accession of Henry Trastámara to the Castilian throne, Portugal and the Kingdom of Castile fought, as the Portuguese believed Ferdinand had the right to the throne. The two nations had three conflicts over this: one from 1369 to 1370, the second from 1372 to 1373, and the last from 1381 to 1382. In 1383, King Ferdinand I of Portugal and Henry II of Castile signed the Treaty of Salvaterra de Magos, which delineated the following principles:

The separation of the Kingdom of Portugal from the Kingdom of Castile unless otherwise stipulated by the Cortes of Spain.

Beatrice, Ferdinand's daughter, was recognized as the "king" of Portugal, and Ferdinand was the "king consort" unless Ferdinand had male heirs.

The throne of Portugal would be bequeathed to the offspring of Beatrice and her husband.

The throne would go to John of Castile, son of Henry Trastámara and his offspring if Beatrice had no children.

Queen Leonor Telles de Menezes would remain regent of the kingdom if Ferdinand had no heirs and if Beatrice didn't have a male child who reached fourteen years of age.

John II of Castile

John was the son of King Henry III of Castile. His mother was the granddaughter of the infamous King Peter "the Cruel." John's reign started in 1406, but he was underage, so his regents ran the kingdom. While they were in charge, they passed the Valladolid laws in 1411, which stipulated that Jews had to wear certain clothing and couldn't hold public office. When he came of age in 1418, John married Maria of Aragon. Of his first four children, only one survived infancy, Henry IV, who succeeded him.

The First Battle of Olmedo

Maria of Aragon died in 1445. During that year, the Battle of Olmedo was fought over the levying of rents from Medina del Campo. These had to be paid directly to John II of Castile instead of John II of Aragon, whom the people felt had the right to them. John II of Castile prevailed in that battle.

John II remarried in 1451, this time to Queen Isabella of Portugal. They had two children, Isabella and Alfonso. John would die in 1454, a year after Alfonso was born.

Young Isabella's half-brother, Henry IV of Castile, was in charge of her when he took the throne, but he didn't take care of her or her brother, Alfonso, very well, despite the fact that her father had arranged this for them. The conditions in their castle at Arévalo were poor.

In 1462, Isabella and Alfonso were taken into the household of King Henry's wife, Joan of Portugal, and Alfonso was given a tutor. Isabella's living conditions were much improved. She was dressed well and had a full education.

In 1467, the nobles in the kingdom insisted that Henry's younger half-brother, Alfonso, be named as his successor if he married Joanna la Beltraneja, whose paternity they questioned. It was believed that Henry was impotent and that Joanna was the daughter of the powerful noble, Beltrán de la Cueva.

<u>The Second Battle of Olmedo</u>

Henry tried to support his daughter's claim. The supporters of Alfonso and Henry's forces clashed at the Second Battle of Olmedo in 1467. Even though Henry's troops were superior in strength, the outcome was undecided. However, Henry agreed to the legitimacy of Alfonso if he married Joanna, but the whole issue became moot when Alfonso died in 1468. Some say it was by poisoning, but it was more likely from the plague or consumption (tuberculosis), which was a very common disease during the Middle Ages.

Ferdinand II and Isabella

Isabella, who had been sitting on the sidelines at this point, came into play. Since she was the half-sister of Henry IV, the Spanish legislative committee, the Cortes, decided that Isabella would inherit the throne after his death. In 1469, she married Ferdinand II, the son of John II of Aragon, which means the two were second cousins. They would become known as the Catholic Monarchs.

War of Castilian Succession

Henry IV died in December of 1474. Joanna la Beltraneja claimed she was entitled to the throne of Castile because she was the reputed daughter of Henry IV. She married King Afonso V of Portugal, who was her uncle, in 1475.

The Siege of Burgos

This siege took place between 1475 and early 1476. Afonso V had his troops entrench themselves at the old castle in the city of Burgos, as it wasn't currently used by the Castilian monarchs. However, King Afonso had priorities in Zamora, so he left Burgos behind in early December. During the course of the siege, Ferdinand II had his troops cut the supply lines and sever the water tunnels. Despite their difficulties, the troops sequestered there held out for nine months, but they eventually surrendered.

The Battle of Toro

At the Battle of Toro in March of 1476, Prince John, the son of Afonso V, practically annihilated the right wing of the Castilian troops. However, the Castilian commanders, the duke of Alba and Cardinal Mendoza, beat the left-center of Afonso's army. Mendoza was strictly a military man; he was just a prelate in name only.

Each side defeated half of the troops of their opposition. Both sides claimed victory, but military analysts indicated the outcome in this battle was undecided. Politically, though, it was a win for Isabella, as the vast majority of Portuguese troops returned home.

Naval Battles

The Portuguese were considered experts in sailing the Mediterranean, as well as around the northern and western coasts of Africa. In May of 1476, the Catholic Monarchs found out that the Portuguese had richly laden cargo ships on their way to Portugal. The Castilians then dispatched five caravels and five galleys to confront them. The Castilians attacked the Portuguese ships near Cádiz, on the southwestern coast of Spain, and damaged their fleet.

The Castilians, under Carlos de Valera, sailed to the Cape Verde islands off the west coast of Africa, where they captured the notorious governor, António Noli, who was in the employ of Portugal.

France's Entry into the War

Once France heard of the succession dispute, it became interested in involving itself in the war and allied with Portugal. In 1476, the French attempted to enter Fuenterrabía (today's Hondarribia) in the Kingdom of Navarre in northern Spain. The Basque people lived there. They stood firmly on the side of Isabella and repelled the French. King Ferdinand was grateful and made arrangements to station his garrison at Pamplona, a major city in the Kingdom of Navarre.

In August of 1476, France sent a fleet under the privateer Guillaume Coulon, and Afonso V also sent two Portuguese galleys loaded with soldiers. Out at sea, the French managed to overcome the Spanish merchant ships from Cádiz. However, the French used incendiary weapons, which got out of control. As a result, the Portuguese galleys, as well as two of Coulon's ships, were destroyed in the conflagration.

Following that disaster, France withdrew any significant aid to Portugal, as their king, Louis XI, turned his attention to his struggles with the duke of Burgundy in France. Portugal and Castile, however, continued to fight.

The Treaty of Alcáçovas

In 1479, King Ferdinand and Queen Isabella signed a treaty with Afonso V and Prince John of Portugal. In it, the two nations agreed to respect each other's borders, and Afonso renounced any claim on the Crown of Castile. Joanna la Beltraneja was given two choices: 1) marry Isabella's one-year-old son, John, when he came of age if he consented to it, or 2) enter the convent. She chose the latter.

Another unresolved issue that was brought up had to do with the competition of Portugal and Spain over control of the eastern Atlantic. The two countries discussed the status of the islands off the western coast of Africa. As a result of this treaty, it was agreed that Portugal would control Cape Verde, the Azores, and Madeira—islands that the Portuguese had historically inhabited. Portugal then agreed that Castile could have possession of the Canary Islands, whose ownership had been in dispute until then.

Toward the Homogeneity of Spain

Ferdinand's and Isabella's accession to the throne marked a time when Spain was attempting to unite the country. There were two issues that prevented this from happening: the Jewish and Muslim populations. Catholicism was one element common to both Aragon and Castile. In fact, all of Spain was predominately Catholic. This was one area that the nobles didn't disagree with the monarchs.

The Muslim Situation

The Muslim taifas, save for the province of Granada in southern Spain, had already disintegrated by this point. The Nasrid dynasty controlled the Muslim population in Granada from 1230 to 1492. Twenty-three emirs ruled it, and for ten years, the Christians and Muslims raided each other, especially on the borders. Battles usually broke out in the spring and let up in the winter. In 1478, a truce was signed by both parties.

The Granada War

In 1481, the Muslims staged a surprise attack on Zahara after the Christians raided their territories. The Muslims captured the town and marched the inhabitants into slavery. The Castilians then sent in a force and retook Zahara, as well as Alhama, which were both fortress towns. The sultan, Abu'l Hasan, attempted to retake Alhama but failed.

The Castilian forces next attempted to seize the town of Loja, but they weren't successful. Following that, Abu'l Hasan's son, Abu Abdallah, also known as Boabdil, styled himself as the new sultan in 1482, calling himself Muhammad XII. At Lucena, the Christians captured Boabdil. In 1483, they designed a plot to rid Granada of the Muslims entirely. The monarchs released Boabdil, who was now their ally, to go to war against his father.

In 1485, Boabdil was expelled from his home base at Albayzín by his uncle, al-Zagal. Al- Zagal dethroned his elderly brother and took over Granada. His brother, Abu'l Hasan, died shortly afterward. Once al-Zagal was in total control, Boabdil then rushed to Ferdinand and Isabella for protection.

In the meantime, the marquis of Cádiz captured the town of Ronda in the western area of Granada. Boabdil was released from Ferdinand and Isabella's protection so he could continue his conquest of Granada. He promised limited independence to the Christians there and got the monarchs to make him a duke of any town he might capture.

The Siege of Málaga

In 1487, the Castilians placed the town of Vélez-Málaga under siege. Al-Zagal tried to respond, but he was slow to do so because of the internal civil war that raged between the Muslim factions. Ferdinand captured the town and discovered that it housed some Christian converts to Islam. This infuriated him, and he burned them alive. The rest of the inhabitants were enslaved. The Jews weren't harmed, as the Jewish populace from another region ransomed those who had been enslaved.

Boabdil took over Granada, Vélez-Rubio, Vélez-Blanco, and Vera in 1487. The Christians took some of Boabdil's land, but he didn't retaliate, as he assumed it would be returned to him later.

The Siege of Baza

Al-Zagal was still in control of the important stronghold of Baza. Although it was costly in terms of resources, in 1489, the Christians besieged Baza for six months. In 1490, Spain succeeded and captured al-Zagal.

Boabdil was allowed to keep the city of Granada and was given land in the Alpujarra Mountains. He was unhappy with that, as the lands were administered by the Catholic Monarchs. In addition, Boabdil was heavily criticized by the Muslims in North Africa.

This land gave Boabdil no access to the sea, and therefore, he had no way to receive aid from the Muslim world. He was disgruntled with the arrangements and rebelled.

The Battle of Granada

In April 1491, the Catholic Monarchs sent their troops to Granada and placed the city under siege. The Muslim fighters argued with one another about what tactics to use, and many Muslims bribed the Castilians for relief. The Muslims attempted to surrender, but infighting occurred because of internal hostilities, causing delays. Finally, at the beginning of 1492, the city capitulated. Boabdil couldn't tolerate living in the mountains, and since he couldn't capture any more territory, he returned to Morocco.

The Jewish Situation

Jews had as much freedom to practice their religion as Christians in both Castile and Aragon. The situation wasn't the same across all of Spain, however. Prior to Ferdinand and Isabella's reign, there were many prejudicial practices in Spain, including persecution.

Ferdinand and Isabella were tolerant of the Jews, unlike many of the other European monarchs. Isabella, in particular, was protective of them. However, with the spread of Christianity, Catholicism, in particular, the monarchs planned on passing a decree that Spanish Jews must convert to Christianity. The Jewish converts were called *conversos*, and about 80,000 Jews converted during that time. Many people, though, felt that these conversions were insincere, so the prejudice against the Jews persisted. Two prelates, Pedro González de Mendoza, Archbishop of Seville, and the Dominican Tomás de Torquemada, spoke to the monarchs about the severity of the matter and how it was leading to disunity. In response, Ferdinand and Isabella spoke to the pope.

The Alhambra Decree

After the Muslim threat had been overcome, the Spanish monarchs drew their attention to the Jewish population. Up until that time, Queen Isabella's confessor (a cleric who heard her confessions), Hernando de Talavera, suggested that she practice toleration. However, when a less tolerant confessor, Francisco Jiménez de Cisneros, took over, he advised her against that. She and Ferdinand then required that all Jews convert to Christianity and passed the Alhambra Decree to that effect in 1492. Unconverted Jews were permitted to take their belongings with them and were given a four-month window in which to do so. If they missed the deadline, they would be executed. Because of the rush to leave, they were forced to take only what they could carry. Many sold their more precious items to obtain more gold or silver. There was, therefore, an excess of goods on the market.

The Jews who emigrated were called "Sephardic Jews," and many moved to North Africa, where they were preyed upon by slave traders. North Africa was also undergoing a famine at the time, and some Jews returned to Spain and converted. Others settled in Portugal, Turkey, and the Balkans. Between 40,000 to 100,000 were expelled.

The Spanish Inquisition

During the Middle Ages, it was believed monarchs were given the power to rule by God. In order to increase their strength in Spain, King Ferdinand and Queen Isabella looked upon religion as the single immutable factor around which to create a unified country. The Spanish Inquisition, which was created in 1478, was used as a tool to create this unity. However, it often created disunity. The inquisitors targeted heretics, those who converted from Judaism or Islam to Christianity but didn't hold sincere beliefs. Neighbor would turn against neighbor, whether out of spite or greed, and many were accused of breaking the law.

Auto-da-fé, Death by Burning

In 1490, two Jews and six *conversos* were picked up on charges of heresy and brought to the inquisitors. They had allegedly killed a Christian boy from the town of La Guardia. One of the accused, Yucef Franco, indicated that the *conversos* took a Christian boy to a cave and crucified him. Then he reported that they removed the boy's heart and drained it of blood. When all the prisoners were questioned, their stories didn't match. Investigators also indicated that there were no children missing from La Guardia. When they were informed of the supposed location of the body, none was found.

Rather than proclaim them innocent, the inquisitors assumed they were all lying and had them burned at the stake. Currently, some people still honor the boy who was supposedly killed in La Guardia. He is called the "Holy Child of La Guardia."

Motives Projected by Historians

There is no consensus among historians as to the motives of the Inquisition on the part of Ferdinand and Isabella. However, a cursory look at history appears to reveal some:

Create an atmosphere of unity through religion.

Weaken opposition to the Catholic Monarchs by strengthening their political authority.

Eliminate the *converso* minority and decrease the power of their influence.

Economic support. When one was imprisoned or sentenced for an offense, their property was confiscated by the state.

Chapter 7 – The Struggling Spanish Empire

Europe benefited from goods that were brought in from the "Indies," the term applied to Southeast Asia. During the 15th century, the caravans that traversed the old Silk Road declined with the rise of the Ottoman Empire in the East.

Spain had always competed with Portugal for domination of the maritime sea trade.

Bartholomew Diaz of Portugal discovered another way to the Indies, so Ferdinand and Isabella didn't want to fall behind. An explorer named Christopher Columbus approached the sovereigns for funding to make a voyage across the Atlantic Ocean to the Indies. Christopher and his brother, Bartholomew, had been turned down by other countries, including Portugal. Columbus, who was an excellent navigator and an even better marketer, approached Queen Isabella. He presented her his astronomical and cartography reports. Some scientists felt that Columbus had grossly underestimated the distance across the ocean. However, Isabella's clerk, Luis de Santángel, told the queen that another country might get there before Spain. This led Isabella and Ferdinand to agree to fund the voyage.

In 1492, Columbus and his crew set sail. After nearly two months on the Atlantic, Columbus landed on San Salvador. Columbus had landed on an island in the Bahamas, although he thought it was the Indies. The first people he encountered were the Taíno, Lucayan, and Arawak peoples. They were mostly naked, which made Columbus believe they were very poor. Columbus reported that they "ought to make good and skilled servants because they repeat very quickly whatever we say to them." He noted that the Arawak people had gold earrings and took them as prisoners until they could point out a source of the gold. He never found much of it, nor any of the precious stones he had hoped for. Columbus made three more voyages over the next decade, ending his travels in 1504.

The Niña, Pinta, and Santa María

When Europeans realized they had discovered a whole new land, the race was on. In 1498, Vasco da Gama reached India, although he went in the opposite direction as Columbus. It was Portugal, yet again, who succeeded in reaping the treasures from the great beyond.

In the meantime, Spain sent out its boldest explorers ever: the conquistadors. They discovered the gold that Spain had long searched for. The Spanish chronicler of these explorers, Bernal Díaz del Castillo, said, "When we saw so many cities and villages built in the water and other great towns on dry land we were amazed and said that it was like the enchantments...Some of our soldiers even asked whether the things we saw were but a dream."

The wonders of the Maya, Inca, and Aztec Empires opened up a treasure beyond what anyone had anticipated. The silver mines in the New World, particularly Mexico, spewed out wealth and overhauled the economy of Spain.

The New World and Its Exports

By the 16th century, Spain had settled colonies in the Netherlands, Belgium, and Luxembourg. In Mexico, Spain owned nearly one-half of the western portion of the New World and the western territories in South America. Spain was the largest empire in the world. In the New World, the Spanish created what it called New Spain, which was governmentally divided into captaincies. Mining efforts continued, which led to large Spanish settlements in Mexico. Cuba had been an important captaincy since the time of Columbus, as was Mexico, Peru, Chile, New Granada (current-day Columbia, Ecuador, and Venezuela), Rió de la Plata (Argentina and Uruguay), and Paraguay.

The two greatest exports from the Americas were silver and sugar. Those were labor-intensive endeavors, so the Spanish sent African slaves to do the heavy labor. They were taken from West Africa by slave traders, who shipped them over the Atlantic under deplorable conditions. The slaves that did survive were sold in slave markets in Brazil and the Spanish coastal colonies. Sugar had to be processed quickly, so plantations had their processing facilities on the same property.

The settlers created businesses to support the cities and towns. The indigenous farmers were given land to farm, and they paid tribute in the form of goods or labor for the Spanish populations. Very few rivers in New Spain were navigable, so early transport was done via mules or mule trains. One of the more exotic goods that were sold included cochineal, a red dye made from the bodies of certain insects that are found on nopal cactuses in Mexico and Central America. Vanilla beans were also grown, and it was quite popular in Europe, along with cacao. The cacao bean was harvested in Mexico, and contrary to what some might think, cacao is not naturally sweet. It has to be sweetened to be used as chocolate. The Catholic Church benefited from cacao production, as it was the most valuable contributor to the tithe, the tax that was charged on certain goods. The most popular alcoholic beverages were rum, which is made from molasses derived from the sugar-making process; chicha, a corn beer; and pulque, which is made from the agave plant in South America.

There was little that Spanish America could offer in terms of textiles, so they made most of their own clothing out of local wool. That, of course, couldn't be used for the export market.

The Habsburg Dynasty

Isabella and Ferdinand heralded from the House of Trastámara. They realized they could secure the Spanish succession by associating Spain with the power of the great families of Europe. The Habsburgs were one of the most distinguished royal houses, having been in existence since the 11th century. In 1496, their daughter, Joanna, was married to Philip the Fair, a member of the Habsburg dynasty. Isabella and Ferdinand's son John married Margaret of Austria in order to reinforce the royal line with the Habsburg lineage. Maria, Isabella and Ferdinand's fourth child, married Manual I of Portugal to further strengthen their alliance with mighty Portugal; before this, Manuel had been married to another one of Isabella and Ferdinand's daughters. The fifth child of their marriage, Catherine, married Arthur, Prince of Wales, before marrying King Henry VIII of Great Britain. She is known to history as Catherine of Aragon.

Although these alliances were important, Joanna played an important role in the destiny of Spain. In 1504, Isabella died, and the throne went to Joanna, the eldest surviving child of Isabella and Ferdinand. However, Ferdinand was not happy with this arrangement, and a brief civil war sprung up. In 1506, Ferdinand recognized Joanna and her husband, the Habsburg Philip, as the new monarchs. Philip died the same year, and due to Joanna's mental deficiencies, Ferdinand again took over, although Joanna still ruled in name. When he passed in 1516, Joanna's son, Charles, inherited the throne, ruling alongside his mother until she passed in 1555. Charles I became Charles V of the Holy Roman Empire in 1519.

In 1556, Charles I abdicated his throne and gave the monarchy of Spain to his son, Philip II. He awarded the Holy Roman Empire to his brother, Ferdinand I.

The Dutch

William the Silent had been dispatched from Spain as governor of the Spanish Netherlands. William, like his populace, was opposed to the persecution that occurred when Calvinism, a Protestant sect, arose in the 16th century and spread across Europe. The coming of this and other non-Catholic religions upset the Catholic monopoly on religions. Because of the persecutions of Calvinists and the heavy-handed control of Habsburg Spain over the Netherlands, the populace rebelled. Seventeen Dutch provinces demanded their independence. This was the start of the Eighty Years' War, also known as the Dutch War of Independence. William led the rebels in the northern provinces, but Philip II scored some successes. In 1581, William ejected the Habsburg troops and established their own territory in the northern Netherlands called the Dutch Republic. The fight for their independence continued against the backdrop of other European conflicts over religion and economy—odd bedfellows indeed. A ten-year-truce with the Dutch was ironed out in 1588.

Anglo-Spanish War (1585–1604)

In 1584, Philip II of Spain signed the secret Treaty of Joinville with the French Catholic League, stating that it was his intention to eradicate Protestantism. Queen Elizabeth I of England believed this treaty meant a Catholic alliance would be formed. If France successfully invaded England, Elizabeth would be dethroned, and her Catholic cousin, Mary, Queen of Scotland, who had a right to the throne, would more than likely take her place and kill her. In February of 1587, Elizabeth had her cousin executed. The Catholics in Europe were furious. Mary's claim on the English throne was passed onto Philip of Spain. Philip was intent on placing a Catholic monarch on the English throne, and in retaliation for Elizabeth's execution of Mary, he planned to invade England.

However, before he could set out on the warpath, Sir Francis Drake burned thirty-seven Spanish ships at Cádiz, forcing Philip to delay the invasion. Philip knew he would get papal support, as the Protestant Queen Elizabeth had already been excommunicated by Pope Pius V for heresy. Pope Sixtus V granted his support and permitted Philip to collect taxes for the battle. Philip then assembled about 130 ships, which carried around 18,000 sailors and 8,000 soldiers.

On May 8th, 1588, the Spanish Armada sailed for the Netherlands to pick up some additional troops. When the Armada sailed through the English Channel, the English navy was waiting. Sir Francis Drake planned on engaging the Spanish from Plymouth to Portland and then at the Solent. The Spanish Armada withdrew and anchored off the coast of Calais in France in a crescent formation. It was hit at night by English fireships. The Spanish Armada scattered, then reformed.

Things were not going well for the Spanish, and it would continue to get worse. The Spanish Armada was delayed because of bad weather at the Bay of Biscay. Four of their ships were forced to turn back, and some had to be put in for repair, leaving the Spanish with just 124 ships. In mid-July, the Spanish spotted the English at

Plymouth Harbor, where it was trapped by the incoming tide. Philip II forbade the Spanish to engage, and they instead sailed toward the Isle of Wight. When the tide came in, though, Charles Howard and Francis Drake sent out fifty-five ships to confront the Spanish. On July 20th, they went upwind of the Armada and engaged the Spanish fleet near the Eddystone Rocks off the coast of Plymouth. The Armada went into their familiar crescent-shaped pattern, while the English ships were broken up into two divisions. Drake went to the north in the *Revenge*, and Howard took the *Ark Royal* south with most of the fleet. They then hit the Armada with cannon fire. By the end of the day, there was no clear winner, although the Spanish lost two ships when they crashed into each other. At night, Drake looted the deserted Spanish ships, capturing gold and gunpowder. Due to this move, the English ships became disarrayed and scattered.

Eventually, the English regrouped, and they caught up with the Spanish on July 23rd off the coast of Portland. The Spanish were foiled by the maneuverability of the English fleet, and the Armada sought out the Solent, which was a protected strait. Alonso Pérez de Guzmán, Duke of Medina Sidonia, ordered the Armada back out onto the open sea to avoid being foundered upon the shallow shoals. The arrival of Alexander Farnese, Duke of Parma, and his reinforcement fleet had been delayed. Therefore, the Armada headed back to Calais.

The Defeat of the Spanish Armada

On July 27th, the Armada was anchored at Calais in their typical crescent formation. Word finally came that Parma's forces had been very ill and wasn't yet equipped for transport. The estimate was that it would take him six more days.

Medina Sidonia waited at Dunkirk but was blockaded by a Dutch fleet, who were allied with the English. Parma sent word that he wanted some ships to push away the Dutch, but Medina wouldn't send them, thinking he might need them himself. The difficulty was the fact that they had deep keels that needed deep-water ports to anchor. Another problem facing the Armada was the fact that Parma's army from Flanders needed barges to cross the English Channel. Of course, that was protected by the Dutch. In planning the invasion, the Spanish had overlooked that possibility.

On July 28th, the English sent out eight fireships, sacrificing some of their own ships in the process. They cast them downwind toward the Armada. Two were intercepted in time, but two others moved forward. The Armada scattered to avoid the conflagration.

The Battle of Gravelines

Now that the Armada's formation had been broken up, the English headed in for a confrontation. The two fleets headed for the port of Gravelines. Medina Sidonia had to stay in open waters because of his deep keel ships. The English, however, had no such disadvantage and moved in closer.

Drake and his seamen fired off a few shots from their guns to provoke the Spanish. They broadsided the Spanish with gunfire aimed below the waterline. Many Spanish gunners lost their lives, so the guns had to be handled by the foot soldiers, who didn't know how to use them. As the English and Spanish neared each other, the crews exchanged musket fire. However, after hours, the English were running out of ammunition, and they pulled back. Five Spanish ships had been lost, and many were greatly damaged.

The Fate of the Armada off Ireland

In September 1588, the Spanish Armada headed toward the west coast of Ireland, hopeful to use the natural protection of that island before going south to return home. After fumbling around in the winds, some ships made landfall in the Irish province of Munster. Many ships were sighted off the coast of County Clare along the southwestern coast. Two were wrecked there, including the *San Esteban*. The *San Marcos*, a ship from Portugal, was damaged on a small island nearby. All who survived were executed by Boetius MacClancy, who was the sheriff there. At that time, much of Ireland was occupied by the British.

At the Blasket Islands, Juan Martínez de Recalde, who had some experience sailing near Ireland, sighted Mount Brandon in an area peppered with reeds. He navigated around those carefully and arrived at a protected area, where he dropped anchor into sandy soil. Recalde sent a scouting party inland, but all eight members of the group were captured. Recalde then sailed to A Coruña, Galicia, Spain. He had been wounded in his battles and contracted a fever. Recalde died there a few days later.

The *Nuestra Senora del Socorro*, a sloop that had been a part of the Armada, anchored near the coast of County Kerry. The sheriff was right there, waiting for the ship to arrive. All twenty-four seamen were taken to Tralee Castle and hanged.

In Donegal, *La Trinidad Valencera* was taking on water. The sailors paid some local Irishmen for a small boat, and all were brought ashore. Unfortunately, they were met by an English cavalry force under Richard and Henry Hovenden and were taken into custody. The Spanish laid down their arms, and the noblemen and officers were separated from the crew. Some of the members of the crew were massacred, but about 150 managed to escape and fled through the bogs. Some reached the house of the bishop of Derry, and he had them brought to Scotland. Thirty officers and nobles were sent to London, where they were held for ransom.

As one can tell, the weather practically decimated the Spanish Armada. Numerous Spanish ships arrived on the Irish coastlines, many of them damaged. Between seventeen and twenty-four ships from the Armada were lost along the Irish coasts. That was one-third of the entire Armada. The estimate of Spanish deaths in Ireland was about 6,000 men.

After the defeat of the Spanish Armada, England sent its own fleet against the Iberian Peninsula. It suffered similar losses. The result of the Anglo-Spanish War was described as being "status quo ante bellum," meaning "The situation as it existed before the war."

The Spanish Inquisition: "The Bringer of Darkness"

In the 16th century, Spain reverted again into an era of purification under the Inquisition. An overzealous cleric by the name of Diego Rodríguez Lucero, also called the "Bringer of Darkness," became the most prominent and active inquisitor. Regardless of whether possible suspects were *conversos*, noblemen, non-Catholic Christians, or peasants, no one was spared investigation once attention was drawn to their name.

Lucero used the powers given to him by the office of the Inquisition to examine religious differences. He targeted Julian Trigueros and sentenced him to burn at the stake. The offense? Lucero wanted Trigueros's wife, so he concocted charges and had the unfortunate man burned at the stake! When Lucero wanted a mistress, he would burn her one living parent and her husband to stop their complaints. When his cruelty came to light in 1506, his prisoners were released. Lucero was arrested, but he, too, was soon released, much to the consternation of many.

New inquisitors were appointed, and they continued to go after converts to the Catholic faith. In 1620, William Lithgow, a Scottish traveler, was suspected of being a spy. Examination of his books revealed that he had placed notes within his Bible criticizing Catholic teachings. Calvinism was the latest Protestant sect that had arisen at that time, and Lithgow was accused of being a Calvinist; in other words, a "heretic."

The Spanish Inquisition didn't deal with many cases in regards to Protestants, as there weren't very many in Spain. The most heavily persecuted sect of Protestants were Lutherans, with some of the more prominent trials taking place in the mid-1550s. One way in which inquisitors got confessions from non-conforming Catholics was through torture. Lithgow was not only tortured, but he was also starved. In the end, he was sentenced to be burned to death. Fortunately, the governor of Málaga intervened, and Lithgow was released, but he sustained permanent damage to his arm.

Aside from eliminating heresy, the Inquisition became a convenient way to punish people for other crimes, mostly ones of a sexual nature. In Aragon, cases of sodomy could be handled by the court of the Inquisition. Normally, sodomy was considered a secular crime, but the Inquisition treated it like a capital offense and issued the death penalty.

The Golden Age of Spain (c. 1580-1680)

Under the Habsburgs, art and literature flourished. Diego Velázquez was a famous painter who followed the heavily ornamental style of the Baroque period. He was a court painter and influenced many who followed in his footsteps.

Doménikos Theotokópoulos, better known as El Greco, was a Greek immigrant who settled in Spain. He brought with him the styles of the Italian Renaissance.

El Greco's View of Toledo *painted 1596-1600*

Francisco de Zurbarán painted the religious themes that were so prevalent at the time. Among his themes, which were instructive, were renderings of St. Francis of Assisi; Mary, the mother of Jesus Christ; and the crucifixion.

Bartolomé Esteban Murillo studied at the art school in Seville. His paintings were very realistic and similar to that of the Flemish school. His work appealed to the clergy and the bourgeoisie. Religious art was prominent in his repertoire, and he painted pictures that were displayed in the Seville Cathedral. Later, he founded the Academy of Art in Madrid.

Some of the world's greatest composers came from Spain, such as Tomás Luis de Victoria and Luis de Milán. When it came to literature, one of Spain's most famous works came from Miguel de Cervantes. He wrote *Don Quixote de la Mancha*, which is thought to be the world's first modern novel. Lope de Vega, a playwright, wrote about 1,000 plays, of which over 400 survive today.

The Decline of the Habsburgs

In 1598, Philip II died, and he was succeeded by his son, who became Philip III. In 1618, Spain became involved in a massive European conflict known as the Thirty Years' War. Philip III died in 1621 and was succeeded by Philip IV. He was a weak ruler, and the country was commandeered by Gaspar de Guzmán, also known simply as the Count-Duke of Olivares, who essentially took over foreign affairs. Olivares was adamant about taking back the Dutch Republic, which the Spanish had reluctantly recognized as a political entity in 1609. The Dutch efforts for independence in the Eighty Years' War wouldn't end until 1648. Since Spain had to finance the war efforts in both the Eighty Years' War and the Thirty Years' War, the economy of Spain declined.

In 1647, the Great Plague of Seville broke out, robbing Seville of 25 percent of its population. Tax collection declined, as the people who survived weren't able to make up the deficit in the country's treasury.

The Reapers' War (1640–1659)

France was threatened by the Habsburg presence on either side of its empire: Spain on its west and the Holy Roman Empire on its east.

This war resembled a religious war, although power and territory were basically at the heart of the matter.

In the 1630s, Spain increased taxes in order to pay for its many wars. Portugal and Catalonia rebelled when Cardinal Richelieu, who had a hidden agenda, urged them to do so. In 1641, the Catalans declared that they were a republic. Spain sent in 26,000 troops to defeat them. On its way to Barcelona, the Spanish army took some cities and executed hundreds of prisoners. On January 23rd, 1641, at Martorell, the rebels of the Catalan Republic were defeated. Three days later, the Catalans scored a victory against the Spanish army at Montjuïc.

However, the rebellion was uncontrollable in some areas, as it started to focus on the Catalan nobility. This divided the Catalans, with some fighting for its independence and some fighting against the ruling classes. Once that occurred, the French were able to take control of the County of Rousillon and the northern area of County Cerdagne. The Spanish border was now pulled back farther into the Pyrenees.

According to the Peace of Westphalia, which ended the Thirty Years' War in 1648, Catholics and Protestants were seen as equals before the law. The independence of the Dutch Republic remained in place, and it was agreed that they were free to practice religious tolerance.

Charles II ascended to the Habsburg throne in Spain in 1665. Historian John Langdon-Davies said of him, "Of no man is it more true to say that in his beginning was his end; from the day of his birth, they were waiting for his death." It was an unkind reference to Charles's physical disabilities and unhealthy life. However, it was an omen that shadowed him, as he was the last of the Habsburgs in Spain. He died childless in November 1700. However, he did have a will and named Philip, Duke of Anjou and the grandson of the French king, as his successor to the Spanish crown. Philip was the son of Charles II's half-sister, so there was a familial relationship between the two. Philip, who came from the House of Bourbon, became Philip V of Spain. The Bourbons originated in the 13th century in France and gave rise to monarchs who held thrones in Spain, Sicily, Naples, and Parma.

However, there was a problem with having Philip as the successor. Philip V was already King Louis XIV's heir. This meant that he would be entitled to the French throne in addition to the Spanish one. This would have created an alliance so powerful that many other European countries would be adversely affected. There would be no balance of power. Britain, the Holy Roman Empire, Savoy, the Dutch Republic, and those who backed the Habsburgs in Spain declared war on France and Bourbon Spain in 1701. Later on, other nations became involved, such as Portugal and Prussia.

The War of the Spanish Succession

France and Britain were perennial enemies, especially when Britain became a Protestant country. France, under Louis XIV, was Catholic. Spain, too, had been united under the Catholic Monarchs, Ferdinand II and Isabella I. The preservation of the British economy was also an issue, so its access to the Mediterranean was essential. In 1701, there were two political factions in the country: the Tories and the Whigs. The Tories felt that the Royal Navy was essential in protecting economic interests and fostering trade. The Whigs, on the other hand, felt that they couldn't depend upon the navy alone and needed more alliances to keep France in check. The Whigs won, and soon the whole country felt that the succession crisis in Spain should be resolved in order to bring about peace in Europe.

The Dutch Republic had been trying to maintain itself amongst the growing powers that surrounded them. It felt threatened by the control of Spain, which had possession of the Spanish Netherlands to their south. They wanted to maintain a number of barrier fortresses to assure the protection of their southern border.

The Duchy of Savoy, which entered the war in 1703, was wedged between France and the Duchy of Milan, which was controlled by Spain. Savoy had historical ties to France, so it was initially allied with France. However, its duke, Victor Amadeus II, was looking to diminish French power in Savoy, especially because England was becoming stronger after it obtained the command of the Mediterranean trade. So, by 1703, Savoy had switched sides.

The Duchy of Austria, to the northeast of the Italian Peninsula, was a part of the Holy Roman Empire during this time. The Holy Roman Empire was a confederation of multi-ethnic countries, which included Germany and northern Italy. In Italy, Spain ruled the Duchies of Milan and Mantua in the north. Austria was concerned about the integrity of those duchies, as it wanted to protect its southern borders.

Louis XIV of France needed an alliance with Spain and Bavaria in southeast Germany to secure its borders with the Holy Roman Empire. He also wanted to decrease the power of the Duchy of Austria, as its downfall would more than likely spell the end for the Holy Roman Empire. Primarily, though, Louis craved the wealth that could come from the New World.

Spain was still in an economic decline and depended upon the wealthy nobles of Castile for financial support. It also relied upon its trade with the New World to supplement its financial needs.

The Battle of Luzzara

At the Battle of Luzzara in 1702, Prince Eugene led the troops for the Holy Roman Empire. On the opposing side was Vendôme, the French general, Philip V of Spain, Victor Amadeus of Savoy, and Duke Ferdinando Gonzaga of Mantua. Vendôme and his allies suffered as many as 4,000 casualties, while the opposition incurred just 2,000. It was a bloody battle, according to historical documents, but the French offensive was halted. For an entire month, the two armies just stared at each other in this area of the Po Valley in northern Italy's Duchy of Mantua. Even though Vendôme lost more men than his enemies, the outcome of the battle has been considered a draw by military experts.

The Siege of Turin

In 1706, France occupied most of Savoy; all that was really left to conquer was Turin, its capital. In April, Vendôme won a major victory in Lombardy, so everyone was surprised when he was recalled to France and replaced by Philippe II, Duke of Orléans. The siege of Turin began in early June, but unfortunately, Philippe wasn't a very competent fighter. Prince Eugene of the Holy Roman Empire outwitted him by joining up with Victor Amadeus. They attacked the French just south of Turin and lifted the siege. By virtue of the Convention of Milan, which ended the war in northern Italy, Holy Roman Emperor Joseph I was forced to grant the French troops in Lombardy passage into southern France. The Allies then confiscated the Spanish Kingdom of Naples, a Bourbon-controlled territory.

The Battle of Ramillies

In late May 1706, at the village of Ramillies in the Spanish Netherlands, King Louis XIV's French army, led by the duke of Villeroi, experienced a humiliating defeat. Afterward, Villeroi never again received an important command, sadly remarking, "I cannot foresee a happy day in my life save only that of my death."

The Battle of Saragossa

In August 1710, General James Stanhope led the center force of British, Portuguese, and Austrian troops. He attacked Philip V's left wing. Initially, the Spanish prevailed, but the assault left a gap in the Spanish line, and Stanhope charged in. The Spanish fought back with ferocity, but the Allies stood firm, and the Spanish were finally pushed back. After less than three hours of brutal fighting, Stanhope's forces were able to seize their enemy's cannons. In the end, about 6,000 Spanish soldiers were wounded or slaughtered. Another 7,000 were taken as prisoners.

The Peace of Utrecht

In 1713, at the city of Utrecht in the Dutch Republic, the Peace of Utrecht was drawn up. It was the outcome of a number of ongoing negotiations between France and Spain and the Allied countries in Europe. The treaty ensured territorial changes would take place that would benefit all the parties. The nations of Europe needed to be assured the balance of power would not tip into anyone's favor. Below are some of the concessions made by the participating countries:

Philip V would be allowed to be the king of Spain, but he and his successors couldn't claim the French throne; likewise, the French Bourbons couldn't claim the Spanish throne.

Spain would cede the Spanish Netherlands and Milan to Austria, forming the Austrian Netherlands.

The Dutch Republic would be allowed to build and maintain its barrier fortresses that had been lost earlier in the war.

Great Britain was awarded Gibraltar and Minorca in the western Mediterranean.

Victor Amadeus II was recognized as the king of Sicily.

Chapter 8 – Bourbon Spain

The War of the Quadruple Alliance

Philip V and his wife, Elizabeth of Parma, wanted Spain's former holdings restored. Sicily and Sardinia were their first targets. Once they realized Spain's intentions, Britain, France, and the Dutch Republic formed what was called the "Triple Alliance." They wanted to enforce the terms of the Treaty of Utrecht and were willing to engage in war if need be.

In 1717, Spain sent out a fleet across the Mediterranean to Sardinia. It was an ideal time to attack because Austria was involved in a war with the Ottoman Empire. The Sardinians were discontented with their domination by Austria, so it seemed as if they would be open to having Spain rule over them. By November, Spain had control of Sardinia, obtaining it with relative ease. Diplomatic attempts to resolve this crisis failed, so, in June of 1718, Britain sent a naval force into the western Mediterranean.

In July 1718, Spain sent over 30,000 troops to Sicily. Soon after this, Austria, which had ended its war with the Ottoman Empire, decided to join up with the Triple Alliance, making it the "Quadruple Alliance."

The Spanish took Palermo on July 7th. Marquess of Lede, who worked for Spain, placed a siege upon Messina, and the duke of Montemar conquered the rest of the island. In the fall, the Austrians arrived to lift the siege of Messina. They were defeated, though, at the First Battle of Milazzo in October.

In 1719, Philippe II, Duke of Orléans, had his French army invade the Basque districts in Spain. They were forced back because of losses due to disease. In Sicily, the Austrians started a campaign but were defeated at the Battle of Francavilla in June 1719. However, the tides would turn in their favor. The British fleet flew into action and cut off Spain from its homeland. This allowed the Quadruple Alliance to score a victory in the Second Battle of Milazzo. They took Messina back in October and then besieged Palermo.

This war even took place in the New World. In May 1719, the French captured the Spanish settlement of Pensacola, Florida. The Spanish took it back later, but it then fell into French hands again. Spain even tried to take Nassau from the British, but although they managed to make off with some riches, they were unable to conquer the British settlement.

The Treaty of Hague

By virtue of the Treaty of the Hague, which was signed in 1720, Philip V confirmed the terms of the Treaty of Utrecht, which stated he had no claim to the French throne or the former Spanish possessions in Italy. Philip V's son, Charles, was seen as the heir to the Duchies of Parma, Tuscany, and Piacenza. Savoy and Austria also swapped Sicily for Sardinia.

Philip's Temporary Abdication

On January 14th, 1724, Philip V abdicated the throne to his seventeen-year-old son, Louis. Some historians believe he was becoming mentally unstable. Others indicate that the French were prone to hereditary illnesses and that Philip wanted to ensure the succession went smoothly in case of his sudden death. His abdication actually occurred just after the death of Philippe II, Duke of Orléans, who was the regent for King Louis XV of France. Yet another theory suggests that this abdication might have made it possible for him to avoid the terms of the Treaty of Utrecht, which forbade the union of the French and Spanish crowns until the death of the last Bourbon male.

However, Philip's son died a little over seven months later to smallpox. Since Louis had no children, and Philip's younger son wasn't of age, Philip took back his throne. His attention moved to regaining some of the territories Spain had lost and to reducing threats from its enemies, such as Austria. He allied with Louis XV, the French Bourbon king, and sent forces into central Europe to fight in two wars: the War of the Polish Succession and the War of the Austrian Succession. These wars allowed Spain to make some territorial gains; it took Naples and Sicily from Austria, as well as Oran, Algeria, from the Ottoman Empire.

Death of Philip V

Philip V was clinically depressed during most of his reign, and as he grew older, they only became worse. In 1746, he died. His son, Ferdinand VI, became the next king and was thrown into the closing years of the War of the Austrian Succession.

Ferdinand VI

Philip V had bankrupted the country. His administration spent a lot of money financing its many wars and well-paid family retainers. Ferdinand worked with the Marquis of Ensenada to rescue Spain from the financial tailspin it was in. His reforms were unpopular and were rejected by the powerful nobility. However, the bank Giro Real designed a system whereby private and public funds were put into the royal treasury. Commerce with the Americas was stimulated when Ferdinand and his advisor broke the monopoly on trade by the companies in the Indies.

Like his father, Ferdinand had a mental illness. In 1758, he was so incapacitated that he was sent to a castle in a municipality of Madrid known as Villaviciosa de Odón. Although his state was described as "prostration," a state of physical and emotional exhaustion, the symptoms that were described resemble that of severe clinical depression and what is called "frontal lobe syndrome," an epileptic condition. Ferdinand was there for a full year—from 1758 to 1759—and it was called "the year without a king." Ferdinand died on August 10th, 1759.

Charles III

Ferdinand had no children, so he was succeeded by Charles III, his half-brother. Charles practiced "enlightened absolutism," meaning he adopted the principles of the Enlightenment, which emphasized rationality. Those principles tended to allow for religious tolerance, the freedom of the press, the freedom of speech, and the freedom to own personal property. Charles attempted to try to unite Spain into a "nation-state" rather than a collection of kingdoms.

The Third Pacte de Famille

The "Family Compact," or "Pacte de Famille," was an alliance between Bourbon France and Bourbon Spain. The first pact followed the War of the Spanish Succession, which forbade the thrones of France and Spain to unite. The second pact was signed in the midst of the War of Austrian Succession. And in 1761, the third pact was formulated.

France was fighting the Seven Years' War against Britain and other countries. Portugal had declared neutrality but was having trouble maintaining that stance because of minor incidents between Britain and France. For example, on one occasion, Portugal had permitted Britain to prevent a French warship from unloading in one of its harbors. Portugal and England had an alliance since the 14th century (the Anglo-Portuguese Alliance), and Portugal had been honoring that agreement. France wanted Portugal to break that neutrality and close its ports to British ships.

Spain had also declared neutrality, but France wanted Spanish assistance in fighting against Britain and breaking Portugal's alliance with them. Because both the French and Spanish kings were Bourbons, France expected Spain to join the war effort. With this pact, Charles III signaled his loyalty to France and entered the war.

Spain in the Seven Years' War: European Theater

In late 1761, Spain placed an embargo on British goods. Britain then declared war in early 1762, kicking off the Anglo-Spanish War, which was a part of the larger Seven Years' War. In late April, Spain entered Portugal and announced that they came to free the Portuguese people from the "heavy shackles of England, the tyrant of the seas."

The First Invasion of Portugal

In the following month, the Marquis of Sarria led a force of 22,000 men and invaded Portugal. Portugal soon declared war on Spain and France. The Spanish believed this show of power would make Portugal quickly submit, but it didn't work. The Spanish were not well supplied, so they forced requisitions on the population, instigating a revolt that spread nationwide. The Spanish incurred heavy losses, mostly from disease and starvation. The British press reported that Spain retaliated for their failure by committing "unheard of barbarities among the small villages; robbing and murdering the inhabitants; and setting fire to their crops."

The Spanish had been defeated by the peasants and disease instead of a professional standing army. But they would soon try their hand again at taking over Portugal.

The Second Invasion of Portugal

In September 1762, two Spanish corps were joined by a French army, placing the number of men to 30,000 Spaniards and 12,000 French. The Portuguese-British troops consisted of 7,000 to 8,000 Portuguese soldiers and a little over 7,000 British. A British observer described the Portuguese as the most "wretched troops" he had ever seen.

The Franco-Spanish forces entered Beria province, occupied several fortresses, and captured the garrison at Almeida. Although it seems like this would be a great victory, it wasn't in the long run. The Spanish were not well equipped to hold onto a fort, and the areas they took over were not readily accessible by roads. In addition to this, another revolt broke out, and disease was rampant among the soldiers.

The Spanish went on the offensive toward the town of Abrantes. Commander Lippe was anticipating this move, and he sent men to occupy the strategic positions around the nearby Tagus River. The Spanish could either turn around and head home or go through the mountains for Lisbon. Since turning around would be seen as cowardly and since Lisbon was the ultimate goal, the Spanish-Franco forces pushed onward. The Spanish forces attempted to take Abrantes but failed. The Portuguese soldiers and peasant population had virtually abandoned Beria province, taking everything edible with them and burning their fields as they left. There was nothing for the Spanish to use, and there was nowhere they could go except backward. In his memoirs, Commander Lippe wrote, "they were reduced to a forced inaction while the difficulties of subsistence, desertion and disease decimated them." By October of 1762, it was clear that the second Franco-Spanish offensive was a failure.

The Third Invasion of Portugal

During the winter, the Spanish commander, Pedro Pablo Abarca, Count of Aranda, received intelligence from British Brigadier General Charles Rainsford, who told the count that the province of Alentejo would be in a weak condition. However, what he didn't know was that Lippe of the Portuguese army was taking precautions in the meantime. He saw to it that Alentejo's forts near the border (Elvas, Ouguela, Marvão, Alegrete, Arronches, and Campo Maior) were strengthened.

When the Spanish attempted to take Marvão, the terrified population begged the commanding officer to surrender. However, he encouraged them, indicating that they could overcome the enemy. And he was right. At Ouguela, which was just a small fortress, the Portuguese routed the Spanish. The assault on Campo Maior also failed because the Spanish lacked backup.

Realizing they had lost, the Franco-Spanish army commander, the Count of Aranda, sent Major General Antonio María Bucarelli to the Anglo-Portuguese headquarters at Monforte with a peace proposal. It was signed in December 1763.

Spain in the Seven Years' War: Other Theaters

While Spain was invading Portugal, the British were invading Spanish colonial holdings in the Americas and the Pacific.

The Captured Spanish Fleet at Havana, Cuba

Havana, Cuba

Cuba was a Spanish colony, and the British mounted a successful attack on the fortification of Morro Castle and captured the Spanish fleet at the naval base at Havana, its major port, in the summer of

1762. This weakened the Spanish presence in the Caribbean and gave Britain greater security for its colonies in North America.

The British Occupation of Manila, Philippines

In September of 1762, Admiral Samuel Cornish of the Royal Navy sent a three-pronged force to land at Manila Bay in the Philippines, which was another Spanish colony. The fortifications at Manila were incomplete and hence not formidable. A storm blew in, though, and the British storeship was grounded, and communications were cut off. About 1,000 native Pampangos tried to defend the harbor but were forced to withdraw when 300 of them were killed. Governor-General Archbishop Manuel Rojo del Rio y Vieyra soon surrendered Manila and the neighboring fort of Cavite to the British, as he wished to prevent more deaths. The English occupied Manila until 1763.

The Treaty of Paris, 1763

The Treaty of Paris ended the Seven Years' War. Spain and France restored all their conquered territories to Britain and Portugal, and Britain returned Havana and Manila to Spain.

The Treaty of Paris is often thought to be when France gave Louisiana to Spain. However, this had already happened in the secret Treaty of Fontainebleau, which was signed in 1762. However, the treaty wasn't officially announced until 1764. In the Treaty of Paris, Britain was given the eastern side of the Mississippi, while France retained the important port of New Orleans. Even though the territory belonged to the Spanish, they had no objection to this, as they knew they still controlled western Louisiana.

Chapter 9 – War of the Third Coalition, 1803–1806

Napoleon Bonaparte declared himself the emperor of France in 1804. In 1805, Spain and France were allies. Napoleon had designs upon conquering Great Britain. Toward that end, France sent out Admiral Pierre Villeneuve, who oversaw a combined fleet of thirty-three French and Spanish ships. The fleet set sail from the Spanish port of Cádiz in southern Spain. The Franco-Spanish forces encountered Admiral Lord Horatio Nelson of Britain off Cape Trafalgar. Nelson was a formidable enemy and an expert at naval warfare. He organized his fleet and rammed it straight into the Franco-Spanish lines. Villeneuve and his seamen weren't well organized, but they fought back valiantly. Nelson's lead warship, the HMS *Victory*, was badly damaged by the thundering cannons. Despite its damage, the *Victory* was able to engage French vessels, namely the *Redoutable* and the *Bucentaure*. At one point, the *Victory*'s mast locked with up with the *Redoutable*'s mast, and the French attempted to board. A shot fired out from the deck of the *Redoutable*, and Nelson was struck. Just as the French attempted to board the HMS *Victory*, another British ship fired on the French. Many sailors fell, and Captain Jean Lucas surrendered after more British ships attacked.

More and more English ships joined the fray, attacking the center of the Franco-Spanish line of vessels, and the combined fleet was overwhelmed. The British confiscated twenty-two of the French ships. The *Redoutable* was not one of them, as it sank in the melee. Only ten ships returned to Cádiz. Although Lord Nelson died, the British won the battle.

The Spanish military garrison dispatched rescue parties along the southern Spanish coast. Wreckage could be seen everywhere at sea. The Spanish Navy was practically obliterated. What's more, the Spanish military wasn't prepared to deal with armed conflicts in the early 19th century. Unfortunately for them, this was when Napoleon struck.

Conflicts with Portugal

In 1807, Napoleon Bonaparte and Spain invaded Portugal. His military force under Jean-Andoche Junot marched through Spain to Lisbon. John, the prince regent of Portugal, along with some of the nobility, escaped to Brazil in South America. This allowed the French and their Spanish allies to more easily occupy Portugal. The Spanish king, Charles IV, made no contribution to these efforts, as he was being silenced by the overwhelming power of his prime minister, Manuel Godoy, who'd been hired by his parents. Godoy created a secret agreement in which France planned to carve up Portugal into three entities, one of which would be awarded to Godoy.

In 1808, the French crossed the Pyrenees and entered northern Spain, taking over Navarre, Catalonia, and the important citadels of Pamplona and Barcelona. Since they were allies of Napoleon, the Spanish demanded an explanation but received nothing to their satisfaction. Therefore, Spain withdrew from Portugal. According to historians, Napoleon had no intention of abiding by the agreement he made with Godoy; he simply wanted to take over Portugal, which had been allied with Britain.

Napoleon appointed Joachim Murat as the head of all the French troops in Spain. The Spanish citizens, riled up by King Charles's son's rumors that Godoy had sold Spain to France, rose up, demanding King Charles IV to abdicate. To save Godoy's life, Charles did just that. The throne was then thrust upon Charles's son, Ferdinand VII, which was exactly what he wanted. When Ferdinand sought Napoleon's confirmation of his accession, the emperor summoned both Charles and Ferdinand to France. He had both of them abdicate before him and then pressured the Spanish governmental authority, the junta, into appointing Joseph Bonaparte, Napoleon's brother, as the new king of Spain.

Spain under Joseph Bonaparte

The Spanish government accepted Joseph Bonaparte as the new king, but the population denounced the attitude of the nobility. The people of Madrid rebelled, and the French retaliated by shooting hundreds of civilians.

The Catalans defeated the French outside of Barcelona. When the French tried to capture the city of Girona, they were forced to retreat. This was the typical pattern for the Peninsular War. Although the French won a few battles, overall, they were unsuccessful at easily putting down the rebels.

Despite this fighting, Madrid was still under French control, and Joseph Bonaparte entered Madrid in triumph and was crowned the king of Spain on July 25th, 1808.

The foreign secretary of England, George Canning, offered peaceful relations to Spain in the summer of 1808, as both countries were under constant threat from Napoleon Bonaparte's imperialistic ambitions. Canning declared, "No longer remember that war has existed between Spain and Great Britain. Every nation which resists the exorbitant power of France becomes immediately, and whatever may have been its previous relations with us, the natural ally of Great Britain." Spain graciously accepted.

Off the coast of Cádiz, French ships were seized by Spain. General Pierre Dupont de L'Etang was marching toward Córdoba when this happened, but he fell back to a safer location. The Spanish junta combined their forces and moved to attack Dupont. Once Dupont saw the size of the Spanish forces, he pulled back and called for reinforcements. While waiting, the Spanish descended upon him at Bailén. Dupont tried to break up the Spanish but failed. About 3,000 French were killed or wounded, while the Spanish had around 1,000 casualties. Seventeen thousand French were dragged away as prisoners. It was a disaster for France. Joseph Bonaparte abandoned Madrid for his own safety and hid with some supporters in Castile. The Spanish troops rapidly reoccupied it and were able to keep the French troops penned up below the Ebro River.

The Spanish general, Xavier de Castanos, said this about the victory over the French army: "This army, so superior to ours, has not only been beaten and routed, but has been constrained to lay down its arms, and give up its artillery, and has suffered the lowest military degradation."

The Peninsular War: Second Phase

Britain started their aid to the Iberian Peninsula by sending General Arthur Wellesley, 1ˢᵗ Duke of Wellington, into Portugal. He repelled the French and attacked Commander Henri François Delaborde at Roliça and then destroyed Jean-Andoche Junot's army at Vimeiro at the end of August 1808.

Napoleon was astonished at his defeats and had his tremendous army of nearly 300,000 men attack Burgos, Tudela, Somosierra, and Espinosa. He forced Madrid to surrender in early December and restored his brother to the throne.

In 1809, Napoleon's troops conquered the province of León and defeated the British forces. Discipline broke down among the British forces, which allowed Corunna, in the province of Galicia, to be taken by the French. General John Moore of Great Britain lost his life there.

The Spanish people insisted that the junta reestablish itself. It was set up in January in Cádiz, and plans were made to recapture Madrid and the territories still under French control. The Duke del Parque, Juan Carlos de Aréizaga, and the Duke of Albuquerque sent out their troops. Del Parque reoccupied Salamanca but was forced to abandon it. Aréizaga lost to the French at Ocaña, and Albuquerque had to abandon his drive near Talavera.

French troops then poured into southern Spain and captured town after town. Spain went into a crisis over this, and in 1810, the junta required all men over twenty-five to be drafted. They even insisted that the Spanish colonists in South America were also subject to the draft. Because the Spanish in the American colonies considered this a European war, they deeply resented that.

Spain never missed a chance to harass the French troops inside Spain with hit-and-run guerilla attacks. In addition to the loss of lives, the French started to find it difficult to keep their supply lines active. Napoleon, who thought that Spain would be an easy conquest, wryly remarked at one point that these conflicts were the "Spanish ulcer."

Joseph Bonaparte

Joseph Bonaparte was a reluctant Spanish king. He was also the king of Naples, which he preferred over Spain because he was very popular there. In Spain, he was greeted with revolts and mobs. Even though he didn't have a drinking problem, people called him "Pepe Botella," meaning "Joe Bottle," in order to disparage his reputation.

Spanish cartoon depicting "Joe Bottle."

https://en.wikipedia.org/wiki/Joseph_Bonaparte#/media/File:Pepe_botella.jpg

During the Peninsular War, Joseph Bonaparte spent much of his time in northern Spain, which was relatively quiet. The French military always checked with Joseph Bonaparte before making any major moves.

In March of 1811, the French forces were down to between 20,000 and 15,000 men. The British, under Lieutenant General Thomas Graham, and the Spanish, under General Manuel La Peña, defeated two French divisions at Barrosa on the Atlantic coast. Between November 3rd, 1811, and January 9th, 1812, Louis Gabriel Suchet moved down to Valencia, took it, and secured a castle at Saguntum.

Badajoz was a hotly contested city during the Peninsular War. Between March and April of 1812, Arthur Wellesley had the opportunity to recapture Badajoz. It was, by far, one of the bloodiest battles of the war, but Wellesley was successful. He pushed inward, fighting a decisive battle at Salamanca in June. After this battle, Joseph fled Madrid. It didn't help that Napoleon pulled troops out of France in 1812 to fight in his disastrous campaign against Russia.

The Spanish and British continued to win battle after battle, pushing Joseph back. On June 21ˢᵗ, 1813, King Joseph led his troops at the Battle of Vitoria. This was yet another defeat for the French, and Joseph abdicated on December 11ᵗʰ, 1813.

The war continued on, but France could never truly recover from its losses, although it did win some victories. In April 1814, Napoleon and the Allies agreed to the Treaty of Fontainebleau, which ended Napoleon's rule and the Napoleonic Wars, of which the Peninsular War was but one.

The Spanish Constitution of 1812

Battles and bloodshed were not the only things to occur during the Peninsular War. The people of Spain wanted to place their country under an organized government. Delegates came from all over Spain and the Spanish American colonies to voice their opinions.

The Spanish Constitution established a central sovereignty under a constitutional monarchy, the separation of powers, free enterprise, a parliament, and even freedom of the press. The fueros that had been created toward the end of the Muslim occupation were abolished.

The Treaty of Valençay

This treaty was signed on December 11ᵗʰ, 1813. As a result of the agreement, King Ferdinand VII, who had been imprisoned since 1808, was restored as the king of Spain.

As for Napoleon, he managed to resurface in 1815, but it was short-lived. In the end, Napoleon was defeated at Waterloo in modern-day Belgium and was exiled to the island of Saint Helena in the South Atlantic, where he died.

Joseph Bonaparte did well for himself, though. He took a lot of wealth with him from Spain and eventually settled in a sprawling estate in the United States.

The Napoleonic Wars and the Peninsular War essentially cut off Spain from its colonies in the Americas. In addition, the people of the colonies learned how to fend for themselves and rebelled against their colonial masters. The turmoil in Europe and Spain's civil wars bled the economy. Spain, which had once been the world's largest empire, was now struggling to hold on.

Chapter 10 – Aftermath

After the war against Napoleon, Spain was nearly bankrupt. Poverty was widespread, as the battles fought on their soil had destroyed farms, cities, and houses. People, who were desperate by their need to survive, turned to thievery and wandered about, taking what they could. Although there were natural resources, the country lacked the equipment and transportation systems to get it to market.

King Ferdinand VII rejected the 1812 Spanish Constitution because he was desirous of an absolutist regime. The people vehemently opposed him. After fighting long, hard battles, the people had grown more independent and felt that he alone didn't have the skill to organize a country in near ruins.

In 1833, Ferdinand died. Ferdinand's wife, Queen María Christiana, became the queen regent, as their daughter, Isabella II, was not yet three years old. However, Ferdinand's brother, Carlos, Count of Molina, disputed her title, wanting the throne for himself. This kicked off the Carlist Wars, which were fought by Carlos and his descendants. The First Carlist War ended with a Liberal victory. The Liberals were in favor of a progressive government and backed Isabella, while the Carlists wanted a more authoritative regime. The Liberals restored the parliamentary government and reestablished the constitution. When Isabella reached the tender age of thirteen, she became queen in her own right.

In 1846, the powerful Moderate Party, which supported royal power, capitalism, domestic peace, and a strong central government, had sixteen-year-old Isabella II betrothed to Francisco de Asís, her double first cousin. It appears there was no love between the two of them, as Isabella publicly showed her love for General Francisco Serrano in 1847. The Spanish were scandalized. When confronted, she complained about her husband, saying, "What shall I tell you about a man whom I saw wearing more lace than I was wearing on our wedding night?" Serrano wasn't prosecuted, but he was quietly transferred by the government.

In 1851, Isabella gave birth to a daughter, María Isabel. However, things were not rosy in Spain. The following year, a would-be assassin, Martín Merino y Gómez, attempted to stab Isabella. Her dress and corset saved her life, and Martín was executed. This didn't end the people's disgust with the regime.

Spain was subject to other political conflicts. In 1854, Baldomero Espartero, who had a cult following nurtured by the lower classes, became the prime minister again (he had served two terms prior to this), and the government attempted to write a new constitution in 1856. However, the government was unable to complete it because Spain was in utter chaos due to the political wrangling among the Liberals, Moderates, and Republicans. The one cause they all agreed upon was the desire to oust Isabella from power. Isabella II fled to France in 1868, abdicating the throne to her son, Alfonso XII. Many thought he would be controlled by his mother's politics, so, instead, Amadeo, a prince of the House of Savoy, was chosen by the Cortes and became king in 1870. He resigned three years later, saying that the country was "ungovernable." The First Spanish Republic was established the same day, and the country was led by radicals, Democrats, and Republicans.

Spanish-American War (1898)

The people of Cuba wanted independence from Spain, and they started rebelling in 1895 after their first attempts in 1868 didn't pan out. Many in the United States wanted to assist the Cubans for a variety of reasons. Some saw Spain as incapable of governing other territories or believed they were unnecessarily cruel to its people. Others saw opportunities to strengthen economic interests with Cuba. As time passed, more officials in government began calling for war, but President McKinley was uninterested in this. However, he agreed to send support to Cuba to protect American interests.

In 1898, the US sent the USS *Maine* to Havana Harbor. While it was anchored in Havana, there was an enormous explosion onboard. Journalists and War Hawks in the US Congress jumped at the chance to blame Spain, claiming they placed some kind of mine near the ship. To this day, it is not known what caused the explosion, but it is thought to have been due to a coal bunker fire, which was exacerbated by the ship's poor design.

The Explosion of the USS Maine

https://en.wikipedia.org/wiki/History_of_Spain#/media/
File:Maine_explosion.jpg

The publicity Cuba received in American newspapers revealed the deplorable conditions the Cuban workers were forced to deal with. General Valeriano Weyler y Nicolau, nicknamed "the Butcher," was particularly harsh. President William McKinley was still reluctant to go to war against Spain, and he suggested that America mediate an end to the war. The main issue Cuba wanted to resolve was for Spain to deliver the island nation its independence. However, Spain refused to do so.

The US used its four battleships, the USS *Indiana*, the USS *Massachusetts*, the USS *Iowa*, and the USS *Oregon*. Commodore George Dewey and Major General Wesley Merritt moved their men and ships into Havana Harbor and pummeled the anchored Spanish vessels with gunfire. The war raged on from the end of April 1898 to August 13th, 1898. This loss reduced Spain's power and prestige in the world. Spain relinquished power over Cuba and ceded Puerto Rico, Guam, and the Philippines to the United States. The US also paid $20 million for the damage to the infrastructure owned by Spain.

The Collapse of the Bipartisan Era

After the failed attempt to set up the First Spanish Republic, the monarchy was restored under Alfonso XII in 1874.

By 1913, the country's political parties had splintered into smaller factions, each of which followed a different leader who promoted facets of either conservatism or liberalism. World War I broke out in 1914, but Spain remained neutral. The warring countries demanded products, which was somewhat helpful for the Spanish economy, but the lack of imports that accompanied the war caused a shortage of necessary products.

Political difficulties were heightened when three political parties tried to overthrow the Spanish government. To put an end to the constant fluctuations between a liberal and a parliamentary style monarchy, Miguel Primo de Rivera took dictatorial power after winning the acquiescence of the king at the time, Alfonso XIII, in 1923. However, by 1930, de Rivera had lost the support of the military, as well as that of the king. He had catered to the elites and heightened social tensions, so he was forced to resign.

In the municipal elections of 1931, there was little support for pro-monarchy parties in the cities. As a result, King Alfonso XIII fled the country, which set the stage for the Second Spanish Republic.

The Second Spanish Republic

In 1931, the Second Spanish Republic was established. Political factionalism was extreme, and people on either side of the fence suspected their opposition was guilty of concocting conspiracies. Even religious attitudes became politicized, as the Church was seen as protecting Spanish values by the conservatives, while leftists viewed the Church as an obstacle to modernity.

In 1933, the Spanish Confederation of the Autonomous Right (CEDA) rose up in strength, and it was powerful enough to quell an armed rebellion in northern Spain. At that time, a far-right movement, the Movimiento Español Sindicalista, arose, which supported fascism.

In 1934, a revolutionary movement took place, which was triggered by the emergence of CEDA. This created antagonism between the right and leftist elements in Spain, which eventually led to a civil war.

Spanish Civil War

In 1936, the political polarization came to a head when Republicans, who were left-leaning and favored leftist factions such as communism, opposed those who favored nationalism. The Nationalists were backed by both monarchical and fascist groups. The Soviet Union helped the Republican side, while Fascist Italy and later Nazi Germany supported the Nationalists.

Before the civil war broke out, a strong-willed man by the name of Francisco Franco had risen in power. He was a Nationalist, but more importantly, having spent his life as a professional soldier, he was an experienced military man. He had witnessed the political chaos that overran the country for nearly a decade, but he preferred strictly observed law and order. To many, he looked stable in the midst of the confusing conglomeration of political ideologies, such as republican democracy, revolution, nationalism, dictatorship, communism, socialism, and monarchy. Others, however, saw him as too controlling.

The Republicans had taken control of the government in 1936 with a very narrow victory. Shortly after, the government moved influential Nationalist figures to distant posts. Franco was sent to the Canary Islands. Emilio Mola y Vidal, the man who was behind the Spanish coup of 1936, was sent to Pamplona. He contacted Franco to see if he was interested in helping take control of Spain. At first, Franco refused, but he later changed his mind. Mola saw to it that Franco was transferred to Spanish Morocco, where he would have access to North African troops. Franco persuaded rightist military officers in Spanish Morocco to rebel so he could gain their loyalty as well.

Their plans were found out, so they had to push forward quickly. The rebels didn't take any major cities except for Seville, where Franco landed his troops.

The Extremadura Campaign

In early August, the Nationalists left Seville and headed toward Badajoz. By August 14th, the Nationalists had gained Mérida and Badajoz. Their next target was Madrid, and it seemed as if nothing could stop them.

The Battle of Irún

Between August 19th and September 5th, 1936, the Nationalists under Lieutenant Colonel Alfonso Beorlegui Canet captured the important city of Irún, cutting off the northern provinces from their source of armaments and support from France.

Initial Siege of Madrid

In November 1936, the Nationalists sieged Madrid. The Republicans were able to hold off the Nationalists temporarily, but the Nationalists kept a partial hold on the University City area. After failing to capture the city, Franco ordered a heavy aerial bombardment, in which the Nazi German Condor Legion assisted. By December, both sides were exhausted. A frontline stabilized in the city, and the bombing became more sporadic. This siege continued throughout the war, only ending in March 1939.

Battle of Guadalajara

Between March 8th and March 23rd, 1937, the Republicans successfully launched a counter-offensive against the Nationalists and their Italian allies, who attempted to encircle Madrid. This was a decisive victory for the Republicans, and it greatly improved morale. It was a great blow to the Italians, though, and to help mitigate the disaster, Franco announced he would disperse the Italian troops, something that he never actually followed through with.

Italian tanks during the Battle of Guadalajara

https://upload.wikimedia.org/wikipedia/commons/8/83/Bundesarchiv_Bild_183-P0214-516%2C_Spanien%2C_Schlacht_um_Guadalajara.jpg

Segovia and Bilbao

In May 1937, the Nationalists were trying to advance toward Bilbao in the north. The Republicans staged a diversionary tactic to stop their progress. They brought in heavy aerial bombardment, but by June 1st,

Commander Fernando Barrón of the Nationalists moved in with heavy air support. The Nationalists' air strength proved to be superior to that of the Republicans, who had to retreat on June 6th.

Between June 12th and June 19th, 1937, the Republicans constructed the "iron ring" around Bilbao for defense, but it was poorly made, and the Nationalists easily penetrated it.

The Asturias Offensive

From September 1st to October 21st, 1937, the Republicans tried to delay the Nationalist advance in the north until winter. However, the Nationalists brought in the Condor Legion from Nazi Germany to help with their aerial bombing campaign. By mid-October, the Nationalists broke the Republican front. The Republicans tried to evacuate, but the Nationalists blocked the Asturian harbors and sunk the Republican destroyer, the *Ciscar*. On October 21st, twenty-two Republican battalions surrendered, and the Republicans lost control of the northern regions.

The Aragon Offensive

This campaign took place from March 7th to April 19th, 1938. The Nationalists pounded the Republicans with artillery and aerial bombardments. However, the Republicans were running out of equipment, as aid from the Soviets was drying up. Republican forces were driven back, and the retreat of many fighters left the Republicans in disarray. Toward the end of March, the Nationalists captured the town of Fraga and entered Catalonia.

The Republicans were able to obtain more equipment, but it was too late. By April 19th, the Nationalists held forty miles of the Mediterranean coastline. The Nationalists believed that the war was almost won, but the Republicans would hold on for another year.

Battle of the Ebro

The struggle to control the lower course of the Ebro River lasted from July 25th to November 16th, 1938. At the end of July, the Republicans conducted a large operation to cross the river, doing so mostly at night. They surprised the Nationalist forces on the other side and took 4,000 prisoners on the first day.

Franco then sent in heavy reinforcements. He opened two dams, and the pontoon bridges the Republicans had built were destroyed, but the Republicans managed to repair them in two days. They attempted to take the town of Gandesa but failed when Franco sent in aircraft and heavy artillery.

The heat of August, combined with shortages of food and supplies, weakened the Republicans, but they fought bravely. However, they were unprepared for the superior aircraft of the Nazi Condor Legion and the Italian Aviazione Legionaria, which overwhelmed them.

The Nationalists sent in ground forces after the aerial assault. By November 16th, the Nationalists had regained the territory occupied by the Republicans, scoring another major victory.

The Fall of Madrid

By the spring of 1939, the Republican cause was doomed, and the siege of Madrid had run its course. Even so, the socialist prime minister, Juan Negrín, and other government ministers wanted to fight to the end. However, Republican Colonel Segismundo Casado wanted to negotiate a surrender. He arrested communist officers in Madrid and deposed Negrín, who fled Spain. Madrid was rocked by infighting, with communists and non-communists fighting each other. In the end, the communists were defeated, and their leader, Luis Barceló, was tried by a military tribunal and executed on March 15th.

Casado wanted to negotiate with Francisco Franco, but Franco demanded unconditional surrender. On March 26th, Franco marched into Madrid. The Republican defenses collapsed, and they surrendered two days later. Hundreds of thousands of Republicans were arrested and sent to concentration camps.

Franco was recognized as the head of state by France, Argentina, and Britain in February of 1939. Germany also recognized him but treated him with caution.

The Lost Children

During the Spanish Civil War, the Nationalists abducted children from Republican parents. Any Republican who had been jailed or killed had their children taken from them. Many were adopted by Nationalist couples after being indoctrinated in Francoist principles.

In 1940, women who were imprisoned were sometimes allowed to have their children with them. However, the conditions in the prisons were deplorable. Children of unwed parents were removed and made wards of the state until they reached the age of twenty-five. Their whereabouts after that were often unknown, and human rights groups rose up to resolve the issue but only met with limited success.

It is not known for sure how many children were abducted. Many children were orphaned as a result of the war, and it can be hard to distinguish between that number and those who were taken. The estimate of missing children goes as high as 300,000.

World War II

Soon after the Spanish Civil War ended, another conflict broke out: World War II. Although Franco met with Hitler, he decided upon a policy of neutrality. This was not strictly kept, though. Franco said he would help the Axis, as they helped him during the Spanish Civil War, but Franco also stationed troops in the Pyrenees to prevent an Axis occupation.

Franco was reluctant to become fully engaged in the war for a number of reasons. Perhaps most importantly, the country had just finished its civil war. Franco needed to focus on stabilizing the economy, which was dependent on the US, before jumping headfirst into a new war. On the other hand, Franco agreed with the political ideologies of Germany and Italy. In 1941, he even allowed volunteers to help the Germans, but only if they fought against the Soviet Union and not the other Allies.

Once the war began to favor the Allies, Franco adhered to a stricter neutrality policy. However, the damage had already been done. When the war was over, Spain was not allowed to join the United Nations, and many countries remained distrustful until about a decade after the war ended.

Francoist Spain

Franco ruled from 1936 until 1975. In the first few decades of his rule, he arrested anyone who opposed him or was known to have opposed him during the war. Prisons became places of death or illness. In 1943, the estimate of people who were killed was approximately 200,000.

The Cortes of the past had no real power; it was just an advisory body. In 1942, the Cortes Españolas was promulgated for legislative purposes. Members of this Cortes could be dismissed by Franco at will, as he was the chief of state and the prime minister, the latter a role he held from 1938 to 1973.

In the 1950s, Franco's rule started to change. It became less violent, although political repression and aggression against his opponents still occurred. In 1954, Franco permitted the Organisation Armée Secrète ("Secret Armed Organization" or OAS) to organize efforts in the French Algerian War since Spain had ties to Spanish Morocco, as it was its protectorate. As a result of that war, Morocco gained its independence, but Spain didn't surrender its control of Spanish Morocco.

When Spain had been occupying southern Morocco, it expanded its holdings in the southwest. This was an area some nomadic Moroccan tribes used. Spain called it "Spanish Sahara." When Morocco gained its independence in 1956, Spain continued to hold Spanish Sahara. Morocco objected to that, claiming that Spanish Sahara (Spanish Morocco) should likewise be surrendered. In the 1960s, Morocco had the United Nations agree that Spain should give up its colonization of the Spanish Sahara; although the UN did so, Spain continued to hold onto the territory.

In 1969, Franco closed the border of Gibraltar. During the War of the Spanish Succession, Great Britain had control of that important region, and Franco was desirous of a contiguous national border for Spain. The people were furious. Thousands were cut off from their families, and it remained isolated from the rest of Spain. In 1982, the border was partially reopened to pedestrians, and it was fully reopened in 1985. The status of Gibraltar is still a hot button issue today.

In 1970, the issue regarding the surrender of the Spanish Sahara (Spanish Morocco) came up again, and Morocco rose up in what is known as the Zemla Intifada ("Zemla Uprising"). Spain suppressed the demonstration, ultimately killing between two to eleven civilians.

In Spain, there had been Catholic trade unions, communist and anarchist groups, liberal organizations, Catalan and Basque separatist movements, and workers' unions—all of these were banned. Members of one group, the Basque Nationalist Party, formed ETA in 1959. ETA was a group that began as a way to fight back against Franco but later turned into a terrorist organization that promoted the Basque culture.

In 1973, Franco resigned as prime minister, as he was getting older, and appointed Luis Carrero Blanco, a Spanish naval officer, to replace him. He was assassinated shortly afterward by ETA, who said, "Carrero Blanco symbolized better than anyone else 'pure Francoism.'"

When Franco became ill in 1974, he had his heir presumptive, Juan Carlos, take over as acting head of state. Franco returned to office later that year, but he suffered a setback a year later. In late October 1975, Franco went into a coma and was put on life support. On November 20th, his family agreed to take him off life support, and he passed away a few moments later. Two days later, Juan Carlos became the king of Spain.

The Green March

As Franco was becoming more ill, the issue of the Spanish Sahara erupted again. In November of 1975, King Hassan II led an unarmed march of Moroccans to reclaim the area. Spanish troops were sent in, but there was no bloodshed. According to the Madrid Accords that Juan Carlos drew up, Spain agreed to cede the Spanish-held land in exchange for a 35 percent concession to some mines there and offshore fishing rights.

Chapter 11 –Rocky Road to Freedom

King Juan Carlos believed in a constitutional monarchy and wanted to reestablish it. He kept Carlos Arias Navarro as the prime minister, but he became discontented with him, as Arias Navarro operated on the laws of Francoist Spain. There was a power struggle between the two, and eventually, Arias Navarro resigned in 1976. Adolfo Suárez-González replaced him as the new prime minister.

Suárez-González supported the king's interest in making reforms, so he had the Political Reform Act passed in 1977. This law divided the Cortes into two divisions: the Congress, with 350 members, and the Senate, which had 201 members.

A Time of Strikes and Massacres

During Franco's era, various political factions had been suppressed, but all awoke and rose up again to gain power after his death. At the beginning of 1977, a right-wing extremist group who wasn't in favor of reform sent an assassination squad after Joaquín Navarro, who was the general secretary of the transport union in Atocha, because of a strike he started. They entered his office, and although they couldn't find Navarro, they proceeded to kill everyone they found there. Five people died, and the psychological impact was great. This horrendous incident was called the Atocha massacre.

The killers were apprehended in March, as was the conspirator who ordered the killings. They were all imprisoned. Writing about the massacre, a journalist, Juancho Dumall, penned these words, "It was a terroristic act that marked the future of the country in a way that the murderers would not have suspected and, instead, was the one desired by the victims."

Independent labor unions started to form, even though labor unions were still forbidden under the monarchy. Demands for improved working conditions caused a great deal of tumult. Some were overanxious for change, while others were determined to keep the status quo. A young man, Arturo Ruiz, was murdered by an anti-communist on January 23rd, 1977, while protesting for the freedom of political prisoners. Police responded with gas canisters, but they accidentally killed a student in the process.

Gunmen who opposed Francoist policies kidnapped Emilio Villaescusa Quilis, the president of the Supreme Council of Military Justice. They claimed to be leftists, but others indicate that they may have been a part of GRAPO (the "First of October Antifascist Resistance Groups"). Strikes were proclaimed throughout most of the country, including the Asturian areas, the Basque Country, Catalonia, and Madrid. Since so many university students and teachers engaged in the protests, they had to stop classes.

Once the PCE, the non-Soviet aligned Communist Party of Spain, was legalized in April 1977, it proved instrumental in promoting peaceful protests rather than armed conflicts.

Finally, Elections!

The newly formed Spanish government had a number of political parties:

The *Pacte Democràtic per Catalunya* (the "Democratic Pact for Catalonia")

The Communist Party of Spain

The Union of the Democratic Centre, a right-wing party

The Spanish Socialist Workers' Party

The Basque Nationalist Party

The People's Alliance, a right-wing, pro-Francoist party

The Christian Democratic Party

The Basque and Catalan separatists

Advertisements of various political parties

The Spanish Constitution of 1978

This constitution established Spain as a democratic state subject to a set of laws, and it holds to the main principles of liberty, justice, political pluralism, and equality. According to the Spanish Constitution, sovereignty rests with the people. The government is ruled by an executive, the role of the monarch is regulated, and people's fundamental rights and duties are delineated. It set up a justice department and a legislature, which is called the Cortes Generales. Principles that guide the economy and finances are also defined.

Spain is a heavily decentralized country. Some communities are considered autonomous, like the Basque Country, Catalonia, and the province of Galicia. Other significant autonomous communities include Aragon, Navarre, Castile, and León. There are seventeen autonomous communities in all.

Modern Spanish Leaders

Felipe González

In 1982, Felipe González became the prime minister. He ran as a member of the Spanish Socialist Workers' Party. Under his leadership, several liberal measures were passed, such as the legalization of abortion, an increase in personal freedom, and a comprehensive educational program.

The Basque separatist group under Herri Batasuna was banned, as it supported ETA, which was a terrorist group. The Batasuna association used to be elected in Spain. It often blocked the passage of laws, as, due to their abstentions, less than a majority could vote on critical issues. The elimination of the Batasunas eased up legislative performance.

During González's term, there was a huge strike that crippled the economy, as seven million people went on strike for one day on December 14th, 1988. People objected to the very liberal nature of the new reforms. As a result, new elections were held in 1989. González was reelected, and his parliamentary support remained the same.

González served as the prime minister until 1996.

José María Aznar

Aznar was elected prime minister in 1996. He ran as a member of the People's Party, which was a Christian democratic party. During his term, Aznar's government focused its efforts on the economy, and it introduced a number of reforms, not all of which were popular. There was an increase in the price of gasoline, butane, and tobacco. Those increases, in turn, raised prices in sectors that were reliant upon those industries. The purpose of this measure was to be able to start using the euro as currency in Spain. The value of it fluctuated, dropping to $.83 (compared to the US dollar's worth of $1.60) in 2008. Once the figures from the European sovereign-debt crisis was factored in, there was a need for the European Stability Facility, which was created in 2010 to help combat the crisis, to strengthen the Spanish economy.

Aznar did not oversee the debt crisis, as he left office in 2004. But memorable events still occurred. During his term, there was a large general strike due to labor policies the workers considered unfair, and the introduction of the National Hydrologic Plan took place, which provided water more equally to all the provinces. There was a reform of universities, the Spanish support of the US war on Iraq (including the sending of Spanish forces to Iraq), and the poor management of an accident having to do with an oil carrier named the *Prestige.*

In 2002, the *Prestige* spilled 17.8 million US gallons of fuel into the waters off the coast of Galicia in northwestern Spain. The Spanish port refused to permit the ship to dock, as did the neighboring countries of France and Portugal. The spill polluted thousands of miles of coastlines, killing fish. In the end, the old ship broke apart, releasing all of its oil in the process. Of course, this caused a severe problem for fishermen and the environment in general, and Spain had to undergo many expenses to clean it up.

In 2004, a large terrorist attack occurred three days before the elections. It happened at a train station, and it killed 193 people. One of the candidates, José Luis Rodríguez Zapatero, blamed ETA, a Basque separatist group, announcing this to several newspapers, even after an Arab audiotape was later found in the area. Various citizens blamed the People's Party, and others blamed different groups. This was followed by a number of illegal political demonstrations.

On March 14th, 2004, the election was held, and José Luis Rodríguez Zapatero was elected.

José Luis Rodríguez Zapatero

Zapatero had the Spanish withdraw its troops from Iraq, causing a strain on its relations with the US. However, he did see an improvement of relations with Germany and France, who were in opposition to that war. Same-sex marriage was approved during his term. The Catholic Church and some conservatives vehemently opposed it.

Before coming into office, Zapatero made many promises, including the availability of more housing; bi-lingual education (Spanish and English), along with any regional language like *Euskara*, the language of the Basques; computers for students; a two-year limit for legal processes; and the creation of a state-owned TV station that is directly answerable to the Parliament.

In terms of foreign relations, Zapatero traveled to Venezuela and Cuba to improve relations. The US objected, particularly when Zapatero agreed to sell aircraft and ships to Venezuela for military purposes.

At an Iberian-American summit in 2007, Zapatero was often interrupted by Hugo Chavez of Venezuela, a situation that riled the temper of Spain's king, Juan Carlos I, who asked, "¿Por que no te callas?" ("Why don't you shut up?"), and left the meeting. Zapatero later made an impassioned speech about respecting the leaders of other countries.

Spain slammed into a financial crisis in 2008. Firstly, it didn't meet the minimum financial limit of a 3 percent deficit limit, so it wasn't able to bail itself out. In fact, Zapatero had to apply for a 100-billion-euro rescue package. The greatest cause, according to financial analysts, was a housing bubble in combination with a very high GDP (gross domestic product) growth rate, which experts felt was unsustainable. It is believed the housing bubble could have been caused by the loose regulations on banks, which permitted them to hide gains and losses. Initially, tax revenues were high, but that was short-lived because many companies subsequently went bankrupt, and the unemployment rate rose.

Zapatero was succeeded by Mariano Rajoy from the People's Party in 2011.

Mariano Rajoy

Mariano Rajoy won a landslide election. He came to office during the financial crisis that had started in 2008. As a result, austerity measures were put into place. Spending cuts were severe, and changes to the labor law triggered at least two strikes a year.

The revelation of a scandal involving the financing of political parties was brought to light. This marred Rajoy's term, along with the issue of Catalan independence.

Catalonia became an autonomous community after the passage of the Spanish Constitution in 1978. In 2017, Catalonia applied for total independence from Spain, proposing that in the form of a referendum. Rajoy denounced it and then suspended the proposal of the referendum until it could be ruled by the Constitutional Court. This move was extremely unpopular. To make matters worse, Rajoy threatened to take over the finances of Catalonia. He sent out police to raid the Catalan headquarters in Barcelona, and fourteen Catalan officials were arrested. The referendum vote was held anyway, but the voter turnout was too low, making the vote invalid. Physical confrontations between police and protestors occurred, resulting in injuries on both sides. The president of Catalonia, Carles Puigdemont, suspended the issue of independence in exchange for having talks with Spain.

The Catalan Parliament unilaterally decided to declare independence with the support of Puigdemont, who approved the passage of a referendum to that effect. The Spanish government invoked the Constitution to remove regional authorities and enact direct rule. Puigdemont and his Cabinet fled to Belgium, and nothing else came from the Catalan independence movement.

Pedro Sánchez, leader of the Spanish Socialist Workers' Party, proposed a motion of no confidence because of the kickback schemes exposed in a case brought against Rajoy. He lost his seat on a vote of no confidence from his party, which resulted in Sánchez becoming the next prime minister.

<u>Pedro Sánchez</u>

Pedro Sánchez is a strong supporter of the European Union and is active in European affairs.

In 2018, he provided sanctuary for immigrants from an aid group called SOS Mediterranee Sea and Doctors Without Borders. They had been sent back from ports in Italy and Malta because of Europe's growing anti-migrant policies. Sánchez's foreign minister at the time, Josep Borrell, said that Spain was looking for "new blood."

Sánchez wants to reopen the issue related to Catalan independence. However, he did warn the people there that if violence breaks out, he will deploy the police.

In 2019, Sánchez's budget was rejected, and he called for a general election, saying that "Spain needs to keep advancing, progressing with tolerance, respect, moderation and common sense." His party won the election.

Sánchez made a major change to the government when he incorporated members of different parties as deputy prime ministers. Today, the Cabinet includes members of the Spanish Socialist Workers' Party (Sánchez's party) and the Unidas Podemos, a left-wing party, as well as representatives from other parties.

In 2020, the Spanish government announced the merger of two banks, Bankia and CaixaBank, but warned that competition must be respected.

The current king of Spain is Felipe VI, and Spain has the thirteenth largest economy in terms of its GDP. Spain has had a rough journey through history, but it has certainly come a long way.

Conclusion

Because of its ideal location on the Atlantic Ocean, Spain has been vulnerable ever since the Iberian tribes inhabited its lands. From all their overlords and foreign governors, the Spanish learned what was valuable. For instance, they learned architectural and military styles from the Romans. Yet their hardy and courageous tribes resisted domination to their dying breath, like the Celtiberians, who chose suicide rather than slavery, or the Numantines, who were willing to die rather than surrender. They minted coins for the Romans and the Visigoths, but they always had the names of their towns or their tribes engraved upon them.

Spain has had its fair share of monarchs and dictators. Today, Spain's constitutional monarchy promotes equality, freedom, and pluralism. It is noted for its autonomous communities, including the historical regions of the Basque County, Galicia in the northwest, and Catalonia.

Spain has one of the largest economies in the world, and it has come a long way since its beginnings as a primarily farming country. Today, tourism is one of its greatest attractions, as Spain has carefully preserved its historical sites and is noted for its beautiful beaches and winter resorts.

Here's another book by Captivating History that you might like

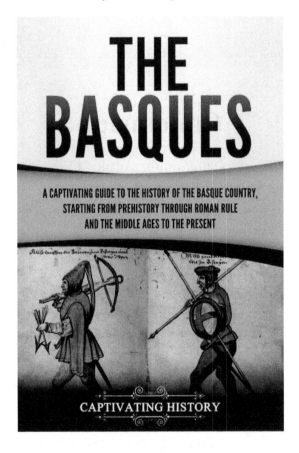

Free Bonus from Captivating History
(Available for a Limited time)

Hi History Lovers!

Now you have a chance to join our exclusive history list so you can get your first history ebook for free as well as discounts and a potential to get more history books for free! Simply visit the link below to join.

Captivatinghistory.com/ebook

Also, make sure to follow us on Facebook, Twitter and Youtube by searching for Captivating History.

Bibliography

"Ancient DNA: Neanderthal" Retrieved from:
https://australian.museum/learn/science/human-evolution/homo-heidelbergensis/#:~:text=Homo%20heidelbergensis%20began%20to%20develop,our%20own%20species%2C%20Homo%20sapiens.

Barton, S. (2009). *A History of Spain*. Red Globe Press.

"Basque History of the World" Retrieved from:
https://erenow.net/common/the-basque-history-of-the-world/3.php.

Braudel, F. (1976). *The Mediterranean and the Mediterranean World in the Age of Philip II* (2 vols.) University of California Press.

Carballo, D. M. (2020). *Collision of Worlds*. Oxford University Press.

Cabrera, M. A. (2005). "Developments in Contemporary Spanish Historiography: From Social History to the New Cultural History," Journal of Modern History.

Carr, R. (1982). *Spain, 1808-1975* (2nd ed.). Oxford University Press.

Conrada, J. W. (1977). *A Bibliographical Guide to Spanish Diplomacy 1460-1977*. Greenwood Press.

Linehan, P. (1993). *History and Historians of Medieval Spain*. Oxford University Press.

Elliott, J. H. (1963). *Imperial Spain: 1469-1716*. Penguin Press.

Hertzberger, D. K. (1995). *Narrating the Past: Fiction and Historiography in Postwar Spain*. Duke University Press.

"Homo Heidelbergensis" Retrieved from: https://australian.museum/learn/science/human-evolution/homo-heidelbergensis/#:~:text=Homo%20heidelbergensis%20began%20to%20develop,our%20own%20species%2C%20Homo%20sapiens.

"Iron Age Iberians" Retrieved from: https://geology.com/rocks/iron-ore.shtml#:~:text=Nearly%20all%20of%20Earth%27s%20major,releasing%20oxygen%20into%20the%20waters.

Kamen, H. (2005). *Spain: A Society of Conflict*. Pearson Longmen.

Kennedy, H. (1996). *Muslim Spain and Portugal: A Political History of al-Andalus* (1ˢᵗ ed.). Routledge.

Lane-Poole, S. (2011). *The Moors in Spain*. Kindle.

"Livia: Spanish Wars" Retrieved from:

https://www.livius.org/sources/content/appian/appian-the-spanish-wars/appian-the-spanish-wars-12/#60.

"New Evidence: Neanderthal Hybrid" Retrieved from :

https://archaeologynewsnetwork.blogspot.com/2017/10/new-excavations-confirm-spains-el-pendo.html#M2UmAL0p8YGlcJfX.97.

Phillips, W. D., Jr. and Carla R. Phillips (2010). *A Concise History of Spain*. Cambridge University Press.

"Studies of Spain" Retrieved from: http://countrystudies.us/spain/4.htm.

Treaty of Lutatius" Retrieved from: https://en.wikipedia.org/wiki/Treaty_of_Lutatius.

Made in the USA
Las Vegas, NV
09 September 2021